Amidst the decades-long general confusion about the most fundamental truths, perhaps the most harmful to souls has been the confusion regarding the reality and gravity of sin. The confusion has reached the point of calling evil good and good evil, and of denying the existence of sin altogether. To dispel such deadly confusion, Father Wade L. J. Menezes, CPM, provides a timely and solid doctrinal presentation on the nature of sin, the grace of forgiveness in the sacraments, and the way to an ever-deeper conversion of life. His work not only leads the reader to acknowledge the reality and gravity of sin but also expounds for him or her the various means of overcoming sin by a seriously engaged spiritual life. A most remarkable element of the book is the abundant quotations from the saints of the Church, which bring to life the Church's teaching and discipline regarding sin and conversion of life.

—Raymond Leo Cardinal Burke
February 10, 2020
Feast of St. Scholastica, Virgin

Fr. Wade Menezes, CPM, has given us a wonderful compendium and guide for mastering sin and growing in virtue. He teaches us to be serious about sin and to distinguish and name the deeper drives of sin. He also sets forth the medicines to conquer sin: the sacraments, prayer, the Word of God, and the many virtues that God gives us to grow in holiness. This book is clear, concise, practical, and very helpful.

—Msgr. Charles Pope
Pastor, Host of EWTN's *Morning Glory*,
National Catholic Register columnist

You do not have to walk around very long before you realize that the world we live in has problems. In his new book, *Overcoming the Evil Within: The Reality of Sin and the Transforming Power of God's Grace and Mercy*, Fr. Wade Menezes, CPM, identifies the root of those problems and leads his readers to the antidote that will allow them not only to survive those problems but to thrive in the face of them: the very Love of God. Fr. Wade combines his own insights with the writings of the saints, Fathers, and Doctors of the Church, Sacred Scripture, and the magisterial teachings of Holy Mother Church to provide the proper balance between the gravity of sin and the transformative grace of the Creator of the universe. This is truly a guide to thriving in this, our day and time.

—Jack Williams
General Manager,
EWTN Global Catholic Radio Network

In a world that has lost any sense of the realities of sin and redemption, *Overcoming the Evil Within* is a breath of fresh air. Fr. Wade Menezes, CPM, has created a wonderful, comprehensive guide to the spiritual life. The love of God shines through on every page. Highly recommended!

—Mary Beth Bonacci
Catholic Speaker and Author

Overcoming the Evil Within

Also by Fr. Wade L. J. Menezes, CPM
from EWTN Publishing:

The Four Last Things
A Catechetical Guide to
Death, Judgment, Heaven, and Hell

FR. WADE L.J. MENEZES, CPM

OVERCOMING *the* EVIL WITHIN

The Reality of Sin and the Transforming Power of God's Grace and Mercy

EWTN PUBLISHING, INC.
Irondale, Alabama

First edition published in 2020. This second edition includes
a third appendix, the Litany of the Sacred Heart.

Cover design by LUCAS Art & Design, Jenison, MI,
in collaboration with Perceptions Design Studio.

On the cover: Adam and Eve stained glass, Holy Trinity Church, Old Wolverton, Buckinghamshire, England (image DT00F7) (RM) © Colin Underhill / Alamy Stock Photo; background (image 1527036152) © Ann1415 / Shutterstock.

Imprimi Potest: Very Reverend David M. Wilton, CPM,
Superior General, Fathers of Mercy
Nihil Obstat: Colin B. Donovan, S.T.L., *Censor Librorum*
Imprimatur: Most Reverend William F. Medley, D.D.,
Bishop of Owensboro, Kentucky
February 11, 2020, Feast of Our Lady of Lourdes

EWTN Publishing, Inc.
5817 Old Leeds Road, Irondale, AL 35210

Distributed by Sophia Institute Press, Box 5284, Manchester, NH 03108.

paperback ISBN 978-1-68278-248-4

ebook ISBN 978-1-68278-112-8

Library of Congress Control Number: 2022931697

First printing

For my Godparents,
Martin and Eldora,
who renounced Satan for me at my Baptism.

And for all those who acknowledge the reality of sin,
and for those who do not: Believe.

Contents

Appendices

Overcoming the Evil Within

Introduction

If we say we have no sin, we deceive ourselves, and the truth is not in us. If we confess our sins, he is faithful and just, and will forgive our sins and cleanse us from all unrighteousness.

—1 John 1:8–9

We have only one evil to fear, and that is sin.

—St. Alphonsus Liguori[1]

1 Quoted in Paul Thigpen, ed., *A Dictionary of Quotes from the Saints* (Charlotte, NC: TAN Books, 2016), 261.

Sin is real. Do you want proof? Look no further than some of the very first words spoken by both Jesus Christ and St. John the Baptist in the Gospels: "Repent, for the kingdom of heaven is at hand" (Matt. 3:2; 4:17). Then, in Luke 3:3, we are told that John the Baptist went about "preaching a baptism of repentance for the forgiveness of sins." And after Christ rose from the dead, He appeared to the Apostles and said: "Repentance and forgiveness of sins should be preached in [my] name to all nations" (Luke 24:47).

Sin and repentance are essential to the Gospel. As soon as Jesus sent out His Apostles in pairs to spread the good news of salvation, "they went out and preached that men should repent" (Mark 6:12). And on Pentecost, as the Church was born, Peter preached repentance to the crowds, saying: "Repent, and be baptized every one of you in the name of Jesus Christ for the forgiveness of your sins" (Acts 2:38). Even the book of Revelation—the last book of the Bible—reports the Lord God saying, "Be zealous and repent" (3:19).

The point is clear: Sin is real. And the need for repentance is real. But this message isn't about anger or deprivation; it is tied to the great message of salvation offered through Jesus Christ, the Second Person of the Most Holy Trinity, Who took on a human nature just like ours and was tempted in every way but did not sin (see Heb. 4:15).

Unfortunately, today we do not hear as much emphasis placed on sin and repentance. There are very few things that must please the devil more than secular humanism blinding our culture to the reality of sin and the necessity of turning back to God. After all, if entire societies forget about sin and its nature and its ability to wreak havoc upon marriages, families, and individuals, upon churches and their ministries, and even upon governments, the devil clearly has the upper hand. St. Augustine describes this phenomenon, which developed even in the early centuries following Christ's public ministry, when he says:

> Sins, however great and detestable they may be, are looked upon as trivial, or not as sins at all, when men get accustomed to them; and so far does this go, that such sins are not only not concealed, but are boasted of, and published far and wide.... In our own times, many forms of sin ... are now so openly and habitually practiced that we dare not excommunicate a layman, we dare not even defrock a clergyman, for the commission of them.[2]

St. Augustine lived the majority of his life in the fourth century and, by his own admission, suffered from a lust addiction for many years. He fathered a child out of wedlock at age seventeen or eighteen, lived for some fifteen years with a woman whom he never married, and likely had other mistresses. Human nature, it is clear, has not changed through the ages. But that doesn't mean we just wallow in sin. The beautiful truth is that our nature can be healed and elevated to new heights through repentance and God's grace and mercy.

Jesus Christ has revealed to us the truth about sin and the need for repentance. Augustine eventually got it: He converted, owned up to his fatherly duties, and began to pursue a life filled with God's sanctifying grace. He was made bishop of Hippo in northern

[2] *Enchiridion*, chap. 80.

Africa, is considered one of the greatest Church Fathers of the early centuries, and is one of the Doctors of the Church—specifically, the Doctor of Grace. Redemption is possible! We must heed St. Augustine's example. After all, if we followers of Jesus do not witness and speak about the reality and nature of sin and the need for repentance, surely the secular culture will not.

We are all sinners. We all need God's grace and mercy. We all need to hear this message of sin and repentance, which is essential to the message of salvation.

The purpose of this book, therefore, is plain and simple: to shed light on the reality and nature of sin—truths that our culture either has lost sight of, has forgotten, or outright denies. Although there are many good books on the Sacrament of Confession, I wish to add to the collection of writings specifically on sin. This book is meant to serve as a layperson's catechetical guide to the reality and nature of sin, to its devastating effects in a person's life if it goes unchecked, to the workings of vice and virtue, to the Sacrament of Confession, to the reality of God's healing grace and mercy, and to the importance of forgiveness and conversion.

St. Augustine teaches that "sin for man is a disorder and perversion: that is, a turning away from the most worthy Creator and a turning toward the inferior things that He has created."[3] Through this process, we forget about sin even as we engage in it, and thus lose a real sense of it; disorder and perversion set in and take root. St. Thomas Aquinas echoes this when he states, "The life of sin is a fall from coherence into chaos." He continues:

> There are two sides to every sin: the turning of the will toward fleeting satisfaction and the turning away from everlasting value. As regards the first, the principle of all sins

[3] *Questions for Simplicianus*, I, 2.18.

> can be called lust—lust in its most general sense, namely, the unbridled desire for one's own pleasure. As regards the second, the principle is pride—pride in its general sense, the lack of submission to God. [4]

In other words, as St. Anselm puts it, "To sin is nothing else than not to render God His due."[5] And St. Basil the Great states flatly, "The end of sin is death."[6] It should come as no surprise, then, that St. Basil also teaches that "committing sin estranges us from God and puts us in league with the Devil."[7] And the early Church Father St. John Chrysostom makes it clear that while certain trials, tribulations, and misfortunes—even war—may be feared because they can adversely affect the mortal body and even kill it, it is sin that must be feared most, as it wounds the immortal soul and can cause it to perish:

> There is only one thing to be feared … only one trial, and that is sin.… All the rest is beside the point, whether you talk of plots, feuds, betrayals, slanders, abuses, accusations, confiscations of property, exile, sharpened swords, open sea, or universal war. Whatever they may be, they are all fugitive and they will perish. They touch the mortal body, but wreak no harm on the watchful soul.[8]

St. Alphonsus Liguori, the founder of the Redemptorists, echoed these sentiments: "We have only one evil to fear, and that is sin." Jesus Himself intimates this truth: "And do not fear those who kill the body but cannot kill the soul; rather fear him who can destroy

[4] *Disputations concerning Evil*, 8, 1.

[5] Quoted in Thigpen, *Dictionary of Quotes*, 260.

[6] Quoted in ibid., 258.

[7] Quoted in ibid.

[8] Quoted in ibid., 258–259.

both soul and body in hell" (Matt. 10:28). St. Augustine goes so far as to say, "Every sin is more harmful to the sinner than to the one sinned against."[9]

But sin isn't just an impersonal failing; it affects our relationship with Christ. As St. Caesarius of Arles put it, "Whoever does evil, does injury to Christ."[10] That's right: Every sin we commit inflicts yet another wound on the Body of Christ, on the very One Who came to save us from the sin that we brought into the world.

It is a doctrine of our Christian faith that we are fallen individuals living in a fallen world, the result of the Fall of our first parents, which ushered in Original Sin. When we receive the Sacrament of Baptism, that Original Sin is wiped away, but its effects remain—namely, a darkened intellect and a weakened will. Prior to the Fall, our first parents lived in a state of justification, meaning that due to their intimate communion with God, they had an enlightened intellect and a strengthened will—but they still had the ability to choose for or against Him. This is why St. Catherine of Siena warns, "To sin is human, but to persist in sin is devilish,"[11] and St. Thomas More, the great English martyr, states, "The Devil's primary enterprise and proudest triumph consists in the bringing of a man to abuse that thing which is best in his own nature."[12]

Indeed, the intellect and the will are great gifts God placed in our human nature. The intellect, which leads us to *know* the truth, should lead us to discover the God Who created us and Who has revealed Himself to us. And our will, which leads us to *choose* what is good, should lead us to love the God Who not only

[9] Quoted in ibid., 259.

[10] *Sermo* 229, 1–3: CCL 104, 905–908.

[11] Quoted in Francis W. Johnston, ed., *The Voice of the Saints: Counsels from the Saints to Bring Comfort and Guidance in Daily Living* (Charlotte, NC: TAN Books, 2003), chap. 10.

[12] Quoted in Thigpen, *Dictionary of Quotes*, 261.

created us but also loves us and wants us to spend an eternity with Him in Heaven. The choice is ours to make. As St. Jane Frances de Chantal tells us, "[Our Lord] never does violence to our free will."[13] For those who willfully choose to keep on sinning, however, St. Thomas More warns: "Among all the circumstances surrounding an evil deed it is hard to find one more hateful to God than the perversion of the real nature of good things to make them into instruments of our malice."[14]

So, what leads us to commit sin? We could talk about many things, certainly, but I'd like to focus on the brokenness that resulted from the Fall. From this brokenness comes concupiscence, which means a propensity to certain sinful behaviors and actions. This brokenness can manifest itself in many ways, from what we will call issues, dependencies, and addictions, to fear, doubt, anxiety, and worry, to resentment, the need to be right, perfectionism, and workaholism. The list can go on.

The great missionary preacher St. John Eudes provides us with a graphic description of the reality of sin and its nature:

> Sin is a cruel murder, a frightful act of God-murder, a ghastly annihilation of all things. It is murder because it is the only cause of death, both of the body and of the soul of man. It is God-murder because sin and the sinner caused Christ to die on the cross, and the sinner continues this crucifixion of Jesus, day by day, within himself.[15]

As graphic as this definition of sin is, let us remember that by God's design, we are called to be free of sin. Even better: Through His grace and our genuine and continual repentance and conversion,

[13] The Memoirs by the secretary of St. Jane Frances de Chantal.

[14] Quoted in Thigpen, *Dictionary of Quotes*, 261.

[15] Quoted in ibid.

He makes that transformation truly possible. What a great gift! And it's there for the asking!

St. Dominic Savio, the young protégé of St. John Bosco who died at age fourteen from tuberculosis, realized the horror of sin when he made it clear that he would rather die than commit any sin—mortal or venial. The boy once exclaimed to his classmates: "Death, but not sin!"[16]

And eleven-year-old St. Maria Goretti, while being attacked by twenty-year-old Alessandro Serenelli, kept shouting to him, "No! It is a sin! God does not want it!" Maria made it clear to Alessandro that what he wanted to do to her was a mortal sin and that he could go to Hell as a result. So devastating is sin that Maria was seemingly more concerned about Alessandro *not* committing one than she was about even preserving her life—and the brutal attack ended in her death from fourteen stab wounds. She died a martyr and today is the patron saint of chastity, modesty, rape victims, girls, youth, teenage girls, poverty, purity, and forgiveness. Praise God, Alessandro Serenelli later repented, converted, and lived to witness about the evil he had perpetrated against young Maria Goretti.

These young saints convey to us the reality, nature, and horror of sin, its devastating effects in a person's life, and the need to repent of it. May that call to repentance reach each one of us and manifest itself vividly in our lives as we strive to pursue virtue and shun vice in every circumstance, asking constantly for God's grace and mercy, partaking regularly of the Sacraments of Confession and the Eucharist, and realizing the truth that forgiveness, conversion, and healing are real, attainable goals. Indeed, these are goals that our God wants us to attain in this earthly life so that we may one day share an eternity with Him in Heaven.

[16] Quoted in ibid., 262.

All of this is beautifully expressed in a passage from the book of Tobit: "Give thanks worthily to the Lord, and praise the King of the ages, that his tent may be raised for you again with joy" (Tob. 13:10). The word "tent" in Latin is *tabernaculum*—from which we get "tabernacle." A tabernacle is not only where we reserve the Most Blessed Sacrament; it is also what each one of us becomes when we receive the Eucharist worthily, in a state of sanctifying grace: God dwelling in us. May our turning away from all sin make us and keep us worthy tabernacles for Our Eucharistic Lord and King, as the Eucharist itself is "the source and summit of the Christian life."[17]

With these thoughts in mind, let us now delve into the reality of sin and the transforming power of God's grace and mercy.

[17] Second Vatican Council, Dogmatic Constitution on the Church *Lumen Gentium* (November 21, 1964), no. 11.

Chapter 1

THE NATURE OF SIN AND ITS CONSEQUENCES

"Woe to the rebellious children," says the LORD, "who carry out a plan, but not mine; and who make a league, but not of my spirit, that they may add sin to sin."

—Isaiah 30:1

God's will is to save us, and nothing pleases Him more than our coming back to Him with true repentance.... Indeed, God's desire for our salvation is the primary and preeminent sign of His infinite goodness.

—St. Maximus the Confessor[18]

[18] *Epist.* 11: *PG* 91, 454–455.

Coming Home

Pope St. John Paul II, in his encyclical *Dives in Misericordia* (Rich in Mercy), has this to say about the parable of the prodigal son: "That [younger] son, who receives from the father the portion of the inheritance that is due to him and leaves home to squander it in a far country 'in loose living,' in a certain sense is the man of every period.... The parable indirectly touches upon every breach of the covenant of love, every loss of grace, every sin" (no. 5).

The young man's hunger evokes the anxiety and emptiness a person feels when he is far from God. The prodigal son's predicament describes the enslavement entailed by sin. By sinning, one loses the freedom of the children of God, as we read in Romans 8:6: "To set the mind on the flesh is death, but to set the mind on the Spirit is life and peace." And St. Pacian, the fourth-century bishop of Barcelona said that "Death is acquired by sin but avoided by right living. Life is lost through sin and preserved through good living."[19]

The great twentieth-century saint Josemaría Escrivá also wrote about the parable of the prodigal son:

> When God runs toward us, we cannot keep silent, but with St. Paul we exclaim: Abba, Pater: "Father, my Father!", for, though he is the creator of the universe, he doesn't mind our not using high-sounding titles, nor worry about our not

[19] From a sermon on Baptism, nos. 6–7: *PL* 13, 1093–1094.

> acknowledging his greatness. He wants us to call him Father; he wants us to savor that word, our souls filling with joy.[20]

This is why it's so important for an earthly father to have a beautiful, solid, paternal relationship with his children: How his children view him as a father will influence how they view God as *the* Father as they grow into adulthood. St. Escrivá continues:

> God is waiting for us, like the father in the parable, with open arms, even though we don't deserve it. It doesn't matter how great our debt is. Just like the prodigal son, all we have to do is open our heart, to be homesick for our Father's house, to wonder at and rejoice in the gift which God makes us of being able to call ourselves his children, of really being his children, even though our response to him has been so poor.[21]

Think about those who experience a conversion or reversion to the Catholic Faith at the age of, say, thirty-seven. They reached the age of reason at around age seven: That's when they were able to start making real moral choices. And yet they don't start really living their baptismal Faith until thirty-seven. What happened during those thirty years? Lousy home life? Divorced parents? Drugs as a teenager? Promiscuous sex as a young adult? Financial and career insecurity? The past thirty years might be quite a story to tell, but compared with God's love and mercy, it's all nothing, all irrelevant. The important thing is that, at the Father's beckoning, the thirty-seven-year-old comes back by making an act of the will to return to the Father. God's mercy is so great that man cannot grasp it.

We can see how this truth can lead us astray in the person of the elder son who bristles at his father's welcome, prevented by his jealousy from understanding it:

[20] *Christ Is Passing By*, no. 64.

[21] Ibid.

> Lo, these many years I have served you, and I never disobeyed your command; yet you never gave me a kid [goat], that I might make merry with my friends. But when this son of yours came, who has devoured your living with harlots, you killed for him the fatted calf! (Luke 15:29–30)

The elder son's pride in his own obedience cuts him off from the joy that the whole family now shares. He refuses to go in to the celebration, and his father comes out to talk to him. The story concludes with the Father telling the elder son: "Son, you are always with me, and all that is mine is yours. It was fitting to make merry and be glad, for this your brother was dead, and is alive; he was lost, and is found" (Luke 15:31-32).

St. Josemaría admonishes the "elder brothers" among us with his characteristic directness:

> It's true that he was a sinner. But don't pass so final a judgment on him. Have pity in your heart, and don't forget that he may yet be an Augustine, while you remain just another mediocrity.[22]

But wherever you may be on the scale, from the lightest of everyday faults and weaknesses and venial sins to the gravest of mortal sins, the choice is always yours to come back to God.

Not Letting Sin — or the Devil — Have the Final Say in Your Life

We shouldn't delay in returning to God and embracing the desire to rid ourselves of sin and its effects in our lives, because, for those who never repent, final impenitence is a very real possibility. The longer

[22] *The Way*, no. 675.

we wait, the more hardened we become in not wanting to return to God—either out of stubbornness, obstinacy, fear, or shame.

The "unforgivable sin" (see Matt. 12:31) is the sin against the Holy Spirit that the Church Fathers have interpreted to mean willful and purposeful impenitence—in other words, intentionally rejecting God's mercy by not repenting of sin. The most evocative example of this is final impenitence on one's deathbed, where one refuses God's grace just before death. This is scary stuff, but it's a real possibility.

Note, too, that this is called the "unforgivable sin" or the "sin against the Holy Spirit" *not* because Holy Mother Church abandons us. No. In fact, the Church sends the priest to your bedside to administer the Sacrament of the Anointing and Last Rites. Rather, it's called the "unforgivable sin" because the hardened sinner refuses that final grace from God.

"Culture of Death"

What can lead people to be so hardened at the end of their earthly lives, even to the point of *not wanting* to repent of their sins? One factor that can have far-reaching consequences for an individual is what Pope St. John Paul II identified as the "Culture of Death." We can see that the Culture of Death the pope described is really a culture of sin.

We could point to all the obvious examples of bodily violence and death—genocides and trafficking and abortion—but we can also look inside the Church. When it comes to understanding the fundamental moral and theological teachings of the Church, the data is not encouraging. Huge numbers of Catholics don't understand or agree with the Church's indefectible teaching on issues of life, sex, and even the nature of the Eucharist. The clerical sex abuse scandals, too, have weakened or robbed the faith of many.

All of this is part of the Culture of Death: "Do not invite death by the error of your life, nor bring on destruction by the works of your hands; because God did not make death, and he does not delight in the death of the living" (Wisd. 1:12–13).

St. Catherine of Siena, in her *Dialogue of Divine Providence*, says these words to Christ: "I see that sin darkens the life of your bride the Church—my sin and the sins of others." And in the First Letter to Timothy, St. Paul writes, "Now the Spirit expressly says that in later times some will depart from the faith by giving heed to deceitful spirits and doctrines of demons, through the pretensions of liars whose consciences are seared" (4:1–2). Doesn't that sound like promoters of the toxic, anti-life culture of today? As the late Francis Cardinal George of Chicago put it: "There is nothing 'progressive' about sin, even when it is promoted as 'enlightened.'"[23]

During a retreat for priests some thirty years ago, then-Cardinal Josef Ratzinger said this: "We are not allowed neutrality when faced with the question of God. We can only say 'yes' or 'no' to God."[24] Whether to say "yes" or "no" to God is the most fundamental question not only for each person but also for each culture and society.

Imagine two panels, a white one on the right side (yes to God) and a black one on the left side (no to God) that create gray where they overlap. That gray portion is where it feels as if we can say yes to God without making a complete commitment. But as the Culture of Death advances, the panels diverge farther and farther apart. There is more white, more black, and less gray. The ability to hedge our bets by staying in the gray is getting harder and harder.

[23] "Cardinal Francis George," *Glorious Lives*, Shalom World TV, October 2019.

[24] Pope Benedict XVI, *The Yes of Jesus Christ: Spiritual Exercises in Faith, Hope, and Love* (Chestnut Ridge, NY: Crossroad Publishing, 2005), 13.

We have to choose the white or the black. Pretty soon, the gray will be so small it will be invisible to the eye, and then the panels will separate entirely and there will be no gray at all.

That will be the day of the General Judgment, of the Second Coming of Our Lord and Savior Jesus Christ. Do you want to be with the goats in the black on the left side or with the faithful sheep, in the bright white on the right side of eternal life? That is the question we face every day when we decide for or against God—and for or against sin. A statement in the *Rule of St. Benedict* (fourth century) sums all of this up well: "Just as there exists an evil fervor, a bitter spirit, which divides us from God and leads us to hell, so there is a good fervor which sets us apart from evil inclinations and leads us toward God and eternal life" (chap. 72).

The Church teaches us about two types of sin: mortal and venial. Mortal sin severs our supernatural relationship with God by cutting off the possibility of supernatural charity—that is, the love we owe to Him and our neighbor. Venial sin, on the other hand, *wounds* charity and thus damages our relationship with God without cutting it off entirely. As 1 John 5:17 tells us: "All wrongdoing is sin, but there is sin which is not mortal." It's important to remember that even when we are no longer in the state of sanctifying grace due to just one mortal sin, God will continue to call us back to Him, waiting for us to respond. Although we might not be able to reach Him when we have cut ourselves off from Him, He can still bridge the gap and initiate the restoration of the relationship—as long as we cooperate. St. Theophilus of Antioch put it this way:

> A person's soul should be clean, like a mirror reflecting light. If there is rust on the mirror his face cannot be seen in it. In the same way, no one who has sin within him can see

> God. But if you will you can be healed. Hand yourself over to the doctor, and he will open the eyes of your mind and heart. Who is to be the doctor? It is God, Who heals and gives life through His Word and wisdom.[25]

Satan rejoices, of course, at every sin we commit, mortal or venial. And so we must begin our spiritual battle by being honest about our unchecked everyday faults and weaknesses—those undesirable habits of mind and speech and action that, unfortunately, seem natural to us. We might describe them as aspects of our temperament and personality—but of course we have a duty to mold our temperament and personality if they're leading us astray. When we act on those bad habits—anger, jealousy, gluttony, and so on—we might not even really choose to do something wrong. And choice—that is, a movement of the will—is essential to the definition of a sin.

But that doesn't mean we're off the hook. In fact, it's exactly the habitual nature of these unchecked faults and weaknesses that make them so dangerous. They dull our consciences by acclimating us to ignoring God and His will for our happiness. And so these unchecked everyday faults and weaknesses can lead us into venial sin. And then unchecked venial sins can lead us into mortal sin. This is why paragraph 1865 of the *Catechism of the Catholic Church* tells us that "sin creates a proclivity to sin; it engenders vice by repetition of the same acts. This results in perverse inclinations which cloud conscience and corrupt the concrete judgment of good and evil. Thus sin tends to reproduce itself and reinforce itself." At each step in the process, we get further acclimated into sin, into the cold embrace of the devil who lies to us, telling us that this is what we really want.

[25] *To Autolycus*, 1, 2.

Also, it's important to distinguish among sins of *malice*, sins of *ignorance*, and sins of *weakness*. A sin of malice resides in (or stems from) the human will, in that the person genuinely "wills" to commit the sinful action; a sin of ignorance resides in (or stems from) the intellect, in that the intellect is not properly informed that a particular action is sinful. Such ignorance can be *vincible* or *invincible* (sometimes referred to as *culpable* or *inculpable*, respectively): the former regards a lack of knowledge for which a person *is* morally responsible; the latter regards a lack of knowledge for which a person *is not* morally responsible. A sin of weakness resides in (or stems from) one's passions, emotions, or feelings not being kept in proper balance because they are not submissive to the will (a consequence of Original Sin).

Regarding sins of malice, Psalm 7:14 states: "Behold, the wicked man conceives evil, and is pregnant with mischief, and brings forth lies." St. Basil the Great, instructing us that sins of ignorance are not to be taken lightly, teaches: "The condemnation of those who know and yet do not apply their knowledge is the more severe; but even sin committed in ignorance is not without risk."[26] And about sins of weakness, Psalm 37:8 exhorts: "Refrain from anger, and forsake wrath," and Ephesians 4:26–27 warns: "Be angry but do not sin; do not let the sun go down on your anger, and give no opportunity to the devil."

The Devil Is Cunning

Indeed, the devil is such a talented liar that for a challenge he will sometimes tell us lies *precisely* by telling us the truth. This illustrates just how cunning the devil is (see Gen. 3:1). The main point here is that in his timing or in the aspects of the truth he reveals, he tries to create a false impression. For example, at the very first temptation

[26] Quoted in Thigpen, *Dictionary of Quotes*, 258.

in the Garden of Eden, Satan told Eve the truth: that she would have her eyes opened to good and evil by the fruit God forbade her to eat. Of course, that was only part of the truth: Satan didn't talk about what God had written on her heart: that in disobeying Him, she would separate herself from Him.

To this day, Satan tries to trick us. When our conscience is pricked, for instance, by viewing something vulgar or sinful on television, he will tell us, "Don't bother to change the channel; a commercial will come on soon." When we are struggling to forgive or to seek forgiveness from someone close to us, the devil might say, "There's no need to repent right now. It will all come out just fine at the next family gathering. Stay silent for now. You don't need to apologize." And any time we choose a sin, the devil will remind us that God will forgive us, which is true, but again, it is only part of the story: It makes it all the worse when we *intentionally* offend God while presuming upon His mercy. For example, St. John Bosco tells us: "Don't imitate those who deceive themselves by saying, 'I will sin and then go to Confession.' How do you know that you will have time to make your confession? Isn't it madness to wound yourself, in the hope that a doctor will be found to heal the wound?"[27] Indeed, the devil's truths are never meant to honor the truth; they are meant to increase sin, to increase rebellion against God.

But there is always a way out. "You are not in darkness," St. Paul writes to the Thessalonians (1 Thess. 5:4). Whether we have sinned venially or mortally, we must remember, through faith, that God is constantly calling us to Himself. In the life of grace, He is always the Primary Mover, Who initiates every good choice we make, Who ignites the spark that becomes the fire of charity that brings us back to Him. But this doesn't mean we're powerless—far

[27] Quoted in ibid., 262.

from it. God wishes us to cooperate actively with Him in the life of grace. St. Augustine conveys this truth when he states: "God created us without us: but he did not will to save us without us."[28] The *Catechism* tells us: "To receive his mercy, we must admit our faults. 'If we say we have no sin, we deceive ourselves, and the truth is not in us. If we confess our sins, he is faithful and just, and will forgive our sins and cleanse us from all unrighteousness' (1 John 1:8–9)" (1847).

The Definition of Sin

The very definition of sin can be found in paragraph 1849 of the *Catechism of the Catholic Church*:

> Sin is an offense against reason, truth, and right conscience; it is a failure in genuine love for God and neighbor caused by a perverse attachment to certain goods. It wounds the nature of man and injures human solidarity.

Later, in paragraph 1852, the *Catechism* describes the many kinds of sins, focusing on the Letter to the Galatians (5:19–21), which contrasts the works of the flesh with the fruit of the spirit:

> Now the works of the flesh are plain: fornication, impurity, licentiousness, idolatry, sorcery, enmity, strife, jealousy, anger, selfishness, dissension, factions, envy, drunkenness, carousing, and the like. I warn you, as I warned you before, that those who do such things shall not inherit the Kingdom of God."

How's that for an examination of conscience before Confession? Paragraph 1853 of the *Catechism* continues with these distinctions:

[28] *Sermo* 169, quoted in CCC 1847.

> Sins can be distinguished according to their objects, as can every human act; or according to the virtues they oppose, by excess or defect; or according to the commandments they violate. They can also be classified according to whether they concern God, neighbor, or oneself.

Who Is Hurt by Our Sins?

It is clear, then, that you can commit a sin against God, yourself, or your neighbor. Sins against our neighbor are obvious: lying, assault, adultery, and so on. But what about ourselves? Let's start by thinking about the nature of guilt. St. Thomas Aquinas defined "guilt" as the loss of integrity of soul, and the soul's recognizing that fact. What this means is the breakup of the proper unity between our bodily actions and our intellectual faculties. In other words, when we act *against* what we know or should know is right, good, and true, guilt is the soul's comprehending that something has gone wrong. And so, while society today would have us believe that all guilt is bad, the tradition of the Church tells us that guilt, properly understood, can be a good thing. It helps us to know when we've sinned, to feel that we have damaged ourselves and our relationship with God. Simply put, a well-formed conscience works as it should.

This proper unity of our conscience and our actions is why we say that human person is a "body-soul composite"—and it gets at how we can sin against ourselves. When we act against the goodness of our bodies, such as through self-mutilation or impurity, we do real harm both to our bodies, as temples of the Holy Spirit, and to our integrity. It is true that the unity of the body and soul is broken at death, but so intimate is their relationship that they will be reunited for all eternity at the

Second Coming of Christ. Where? Heaven or Hell. This is the truth of our Faith.

Let's also consider how we can sin against God. The most obvious example is blasphemy, such as using His name in vain. A priest may commit blasphemy—that is, treating the name and reality of God disrespectfully—by celebrating an irreverent Liturgy by ignoring or adding to the proper rubrics of the Mass. In so doing, the priest makes Holy Mass his own personal stage. Vatican II tells us that the Sacred Liturgy is, above all, the solemn worship of the Divine Majesty.[29] Turning the Mass into a priest show distracts from that majesty, and it is therefore a sin against God.

The *Catechism* says that sins "can be divided into spiritual or carnal sins, or again as sins in thought, word, deed, or omission" (1853). A sin of *omission* is the failure to do something that you are morally bound to do. For instance, if your friend tells you she is going to have an abortion and you remain silent, that is a sin of omission. You're not bound to restrain her physically, but you must take the opportunity to evangelize, to speak the truth to her in charity. Driving her to the abortion clinic, on the other hand, would be a sin of *commission*, by which you take part in her sin. Thus, a sin of commission is to do something (immoral) that you should *not* do. The *Catechism* tells us further:

> The root of sin is in the heart of man, in his free will, according to the teaching of the Lord: "For out of the heart come evil thoughts, murder, adultery, fornication, theft, false witness and slander. These are what defile a man" (Matt. 15:19–20). But in the heart also resides charity, the source of the good and pure works, which sin wounds.

[29] Second Vatican Council, Constitution on the Sacred Liturgy *Sacrosanctum Concilium* (December 4, 1963), no. 33.

Sins are rightly evaluated according to their gravity. The distinction between mortal and venial sin, already evident in Scripture (cf. 1 John 5:16–17), became part of the tradition of the Church. It is corroborated by human experience. (1853–1854)

We have already described the effects of mortal sin, but what makes a sin mortal? Mortal sin requires three conditions: grave matter, full knowledge, and deliberate consent of the will. That is, the content of the sin must be serious, we must know it is seriously sinful, and we must choose to commit the sin without being coerced in any way. If any one of these three elements is missing, then the sin is venial, not mortal; it wounds but does not break our supernatural relationship with God. Regarding deliberate consent of the will, a distinction must be made between *voluntary* and *involuntary* moral actions. With voluntary actions, one has control of one's free will and choice; what is voluntary *is* morally imputable. Involuntary actions are not under the control of one's free will and choice; what is involuntary *is not* morally imputable. It should be noted, too, that Catholic moral theology recognizes six primary hindrances to full imputability: ignorance, fear, passion, habits, violence, and mental disorder. Also, in discerning the morality of human acts, the "sources" or constitutive elements of *object*, *intention*, and *circumstance* must also be taken into consideration.[30]

Let us remember, too, that sin, whether venial or mortal, is *always* a personal act. We might commit it with another, as in adultery or robbing a bank, but it is still a personal act for which we bear personal responsibility. The *Catechism* conveys this truth clearly:

> Sin is a personal act. Moreover, we have a responsibility for the sins committed by others when we cooperate in them: by participating directly and voluntarily in them; by ordering,

[30] See CCC 1749–1761.

> advising, praising, or approving them; by not disclosing or not hindering them when we have an obligation to do so; by protecting evil-doers. (1868)

As to this last point, we can easily discern a grave failure on the part of the human element of the Church's hierarchy regarding the clerical abuse scandals.

Let us remember, too, that from personal sin come "structures of sin" in society. Also called "social sin," "structures of sin" refers to the effect of sin over time that can corrupt society and its institutions. For example, we can see this in laws at all governmental levels that go against both natural and divine law, such as permitting abortion, euthanasia, and unnatural marriage. The *Catechism* states:

> Sin makes men accomplices of one another and causes concupiscence, violence, and injustice to reign among them. Sins give rise to social situations and institutions that are contrary to the divine goodness. "Structures of sin" are the expression and effect of personal sins. They lead their victims to do evil in their turn. In an analogous sense, they constitute a "social sin."[31] (1869)

Four Consequences of Sin

The Church also teaches that there are four consequences of sin:[32] *personal*, *social*, *ecclesial*, and *cosmic*. In other words, each and every sin committed affects the sinner in his relationship with himself (as we've discussed), in his relationship with others,

[31] Quoting Pope St. John Paul II, apostolic exhortation *Reconciliatio et paenitentia* (December 2, 1984), no. 16.

[32] See CCC 1469.

in his relationship with the entire Body of Christ, and in his relationship with God and all of creation. Read chapter 3 of Genesis to see how creation was disrupted by the sin of our first parents. The good news, however, is that these four areas of disruption and disintegration are healed in the Sacrament of Reconciliation through Almighty God's divine intervention. Pope St. John Paul II's landmark apostolic exhortation *On Reconciliation and Penance* conveys this truth:

> It must be recalled that ... this reconciliation with God leads, as it were, to other reconciliations, which repair the other breaches caused by sin. The forgiven penitent is reconciled with *himself* in his inmost being, where he regains his innermost truth. He is reconciled with his *brethren* whom he has in some way offended and wounded. He is reconciled with the *Church*. He is reconciled with all *creation*."[33]

The Confession of Sins

Confession of one's sins should be done in a simple, concise manner. Mortal sins must be confessed in their kind and approximate number. Any aggravating circumstances that make a mortal sin objectively graver should be included but still mentioned simply—without a lot of great or graphic detail, which the sacrament does not ask for. Show me a person who is afraid of Confession, and I will show you someone who believes he has to go into great and graphic detail about his sins. But this is not what the Church requires.

Sound teaching gives two reasons why penitents should not go into great or graphic detail about their individual sins: first, lest the

[33] *Reconciliatio et paenitentia*, 31, 5, quoted in CCC 1469; emphasis added.

penitents lead themselves into scrupulosity precisely by habitually confessing every single detail all the time; and, second, lest the penitents lead the confessor into sins of thought by describing their transgressions so graphically. In other words, the penitent has a moral duty and responsibility to protect the thought processes of the confessor. Even though the confessor is administrating the Sacrament of Confession *in persona Christi* (in the person of Christ) and as an *alter Christus* (another Christ), he is still a human being subject to weakness. Also, although a confessor has a right to question a penitent in the confessional—for example, to gain a better understanding of a confessed sin—such questions should never hint at a morbid curiosity or grave delectation on the part of the confessor. If they do, the penitent should graciously end the sacrament by excusing himself.

Venial sins, unlike mortal sins, can be forgiven outside the Sacrament of Confession—specifically, by praying a fervent Act of Contrition or by making a good and holy Communion. This is why an examination of conscience, traditionally done twice each day—at midday (the *particular examen*) and at the end of the day (the *general examen*)—is so important, because each examination of conscience ends with an Act of Contrition. We must remember, as we talk about Confession and forgiveness, that God is always our Primary Mover, whether or not we are in a state of grace. When we go to Confession or pray an Act of Contrition, we are responding to the movement of grace in our hearts.

Confessing venial sins, though not required, is nevertheless strongly recommended by Holy Mother Church because doing so helps one to fight against evil tendencies and to form a correct conscience. "Deliberate and unrepented venial sin disposes us little by little to commit mortal sin" (CCC 1863). God's sanctifying grace comes through the sacraments, so if we bring our venial sins to Confession, we have the moral certitude that grace is increased in us.

Benefits of Frequent Confession

What are some of the benefits of a good, holy, regular Confession—say, once a month or so? Well, quite simply, the grace of the sacrament can protect us from sin by strengthening our resolve and reforming our habits. The Church's law states that we must go to Confession once a year if we are conscious of mortal sin. But even better is the time-honored tradition of going monthly. In fact, show me a faithful, monthly penitent, and chances are that person never has mortal sin to confess: It is precisely the person's monthly Confession, done faithfully and fervently, that keeps him from committing mortal sin.

Pope Pius XII recommended the practice of frequent Confession—even of venial sins:

> By it, self-knowledge is increased, Christian humility grows, bad habits are corrected, spiritual neglect and tepidity are resisted, the conscience is purified, the will is strengthened, a salutary self-control is attained, and grace is increased in virtue of the Sacrament itself.[34]

Also, in promulgating the new rite of the Sacrament of Penance following the Second Vatican Council, Pope St. Paul VI emphasized the "great value" of "frequent and reverent recourse to this Sacrament (of Confession) even when only venial sins are in question." This practice "is a constant effort to bring to perfection the grace of our Baptism."[35]

St. Isidore of Seville says that "confession heals, confession justifies, confession grants pardon of sin. All hope consists in confession.

[34] Pope Pius XII, encyclical *Mystici Corporis Christi* (June 29, 1943), no. 88.

[35] Accompanying the promulgation of the *Ordo Paenitentiae*, December 2, 1973.

In confession there is a chance for mercy. Believe it firmly. Do not doubt, do not hesitate, never despair of the mercy of God. Hope and have confidence in confession."[36] Hope and have confidence in Confession just as that younger son did when he returned to his father. In that famous Gospel parable, remember when his father saw him at a distance and ran out to greet him and embrace him with a kiss? This is what happens to our souls when we approach the confessional. How beautifully that parable applies to each one of us and to that sacrament of mercy.

St. Faustina Kowalska, the Divine Mercy seer, recorded these words of Our Lord in her *Diary*:

> Write, speak of My mercy. Tell souls where they are to look for solace; that is, in the Tribunal of Mercy [the Sacrament of Reconciliation]. There the greatest miracles take place [and] are incessantly repeated. To avail oneself of this miracle, it is not necessary to go on a great pilgrimage or to carry out some external ceremony; it suffices to come with faith to the feet of My representative and to reveal to him one's misery, and the miracle of Divine Mercy will be fully demonstrated. Were a soul like a decaying corpse so that from a human standpoint, there would be no [hope of] restoration and everything would already be lost, it is not so with God. The miracle of Divine Mercy restores that soul in full. Oh, how miserable are those who do not take advantage of the miracle of God's mercy! They will call out in vain, but it will be too late. (1448)

St. Claude de la Colombière, the spiritual director of St. Margaret Mary Alacoque, said that "of all the confidence that exists, that

[36] Quoted in Mike Aquilina, *The Way of the Fathers: Praying with the Early Christians* (Huntington, IN: Our Sunday Visitor, 1999), 67.

which most honors the Lord is the confidence of the most notorious sinner who is so convinced of God's infinite mercy that all his sins seem to him as but an atom in the presence of This Mercy."[37] The word "confidence" comes from the Latin *con* and *fide*: "with faith." We have faith that God calls us back to Himself every time we stray. He wants us, individually, to be active instruments of His will by responding to His promptings of grace.

Later in her *Diary*, St. Faustina recorded these words of Our Lord:

> My daughter, do not tire of proclaiming My mercy. In this way you will refresh this Heart of Mine, which burns with the flame of pity for sinners. Tell My priests that hardened sinners will repent upon hearing their words when they speak about My unfathomable mercy, about the compassion I have for them in My Heart. To priests who proclaim and extol My mercy, I will give wondrous power; I will anoint their words and touch the hearts of those to whom they will speak. (1521)

Many of the Church Fathers note that mercy is God's greatest attribute: What a gift we have in His mercy! Indeed, we can say that mercy is who God is. It's Love's second name. Why? Because God is more interested in our future than in our past; He's more interested in the kind of person we can *yet* become than in the kind of person we *used* to be. While indeed taking our sins seriously because they have either wounded or severed our supernatural relationship with Him, God never, ever takes those sins as the last word. Why? Because He has made us in His image and likeness (Gen. 1:26–27); He calls us to a life of His sanctifying grace; and

[37] Quoted in Jim Manney, *An Ignatian Book of Days* (Chicago: Loyola Press, 2014), February 17.

He is our God, Who is bigger than any sin we might ever commit, even the most hideous and wicked mortal sin.

And yet we must examine ourselves, as St. Augustine asks: "Are we really certain that we love Him? Or, do we love our sins more? Therefore, let us hate our sins and love Him Who will exact punishment for them."[38] Again, though, that punishment is never, ever the last word. God sees our sins for what they are, but at the same time He knows that there is much more to us than those sins. God will help each one of us patiently to grow into the person He wants us to become. He is willing to do this saving work within us, if only we let Him enter into our lives. After all, this is what He called us to from the moment of creation, when we were made in His image and likeness. He calls us to a life in His sanctifying grace, which makes us actual participators in His divine life.

Isaiah 45:22 says, "Turn to me and be saved." I love reading this short passage over and over again when I make a visit to the Blessed Sacrament. I simply look at the sanctuary lamp—the flame that symbolizes the true, real, abiding, substantial Living Presence of Christ in the Eucharist, in His Body, Blood, Soul, and Divinity. He is always there. He is a constant, just waiting for us to turn to Him—and away from our sin—and be saved.

Now that we've discussed the nature of sin and its consequences, let us examine the subjects of virtue, vice, and the importance of growing in self-knowledge—precisely to overcome sin.

[38] Discourse on the Psalms.

Chapter 2

Know Thyself: Virtue, Vice, and Growth in Self-Knowledge

The grace of God has appeared, offering salvation to all men. It trains us to reject godless ways and worldly desires, and live temperately, justly and devoutly in this age.

—Titus 2:11–12

Keep on making progress. This progress, however, must be in virtue; for there are some, the Apostle warns, whose only progress is in vice. If you make progress, you will be continuing your journey, but be sure that your progress is in virtue, true faith, and right living.

—St. Augustine[39]

[39] *Sermo* 256, 1.2.3: *PL* 38, 1191–1193.

Issues, Dependencies, and Addictions

We often find ourselves caught up in any variety of issues, dependencies, and addictions that can keep us from a supernatural love of both God and neighbor. Now, in talking about these categories, let me note that I am not a clinical psychologist; rather, I am a Catholic priest who is a member of an itinerant missionary preaching order, and as part of the charism of that order, I hear many confessions. And so what follows is simply a *pastoral perspective* on these three categories.

An "issue," as used here, may be said to be a strong feeling or view that you hold toward a person, place, or thing. While you might hold on to this issue firmly and strongly, it is generally fleeting in its control over you. That is, it does not interfere directly with your everyday activities and affairs. A classic example would be something like this: "I haven't talked to my sister-in-law in twenty-five years because during a Thanksgiving Day dinner, she chewed me out in front of my other relatives." So, you don't think about your sister-in-law every day; your everyday life proceeds normally. But when you *do* think about her, you feel angry. Well, whether you want to admit it or not, for the past twenty-five years, that sister-in-law has had some control over you, because someone who angers you controls you. If just thinking about her brings up this unbidden emotion, she has control.

For purposes of this discussion, one can be said to develop a "dependency" on a person, place, or thing whenever he comes to rely on it for his concept of his self-worth or day-to-day functioning.

In other words, if you don't have this person, place, or thing in your life, you feel as if your life loses its meaning, and you find it difficult to carry out regular tasks. A dependency is something that consumes you primarily psychologically, as opposed to an addiction, which can become a biological necessity as well. But, of course, a dependency, especially if it involves a substance such as alcohol or nicotine, can become an addiction. An example of a dependency would be an abusive relationship, in which a young woman feels that from her cruel boyfriend she receives her self-worth. Her friends tell her how abusive he is, and yet she just can't break up with him. She can't see what her friends, who are outside the relationship, *can* see.

An addiction, as mentioned here, can also involve a person, place, or thing, but it usually involves a substance or a severe vice such as lust, gambling, or alcohol. It is something that you have grown to need on a nearly daily basis in order to function. You feel as if you will lose control of your life if your craving can't be satisfied, even though, of course, this is the very thing that is destroying you. Addictions usually begin as dependencies, which can then become acquired biological necessities, where the body cannot survive without the craved substance. This is why we have detox programs: A person has to be weaned off heroin, for example, because the body will crash without it.

Having looked at how issues, dependencies and addictions can adversely affect our everyday lives in our relationships with God and others, let's look a bit further at just one example of how these play out: the unwillingness to forgive. Experience demonstrates that the effects of an unwillingness to forgive are so devastating that they can make life torturous. We can see this at the end of the parable of the unforgiving servant:

> Then his lord summoned him and said to him, "You wicked servant! I forgave you all that debt because you besought me;

> and should not you have had mercy on your fellow servant, as I had mercy on you?" And in anger his lord delivered him to the jailers, till he should pay all his debt. So also my heavenly Father will do to every one of you, if you do not forgive your brother from your heart." (Matt. 18:33–36)

Forgiveness, on the other hand, makes our lives miraculous and full of grace. By choosing to forgive, we choose the life of mercy and grace that God has made us for, rather than a life of deprivation and torture. "Forgive your neighbor the wrong he has done, and then your sins will be pardoned when you pray" (Sir. 28:2).

St. Paul wrote, "None of us lives to himself, and none of us dies to himself. If we live, we live to the Lord, and if we die, we die to the Lord; so then, whether we live or whether we die, we are the Lord's" (Rom. 14:7-8). The Lord Himself wants us to receive and practice mercy, love, and forgiveness. From these, we receive life in Christ; without them, we are separated from Him. Yet the devil would like nothing more than to tempt us *not* to forgive. And while such temptations can be strong and enduring, we need to turn to God willfully, seeking to do His will, and hold strong until the temptation dissipates.

St. Faustina once described a time of strong temptation like this:

> I remained silent, and by an act of will I dwelt in God, although a moan escaped from my heart. Finally, the tempter went away and I, exhausted, fell asleep immediately. In the morning, right after receiving Holy Communion, I went immediately to my cell and falling on my knees I renewed my act of submission in all things to the will of God. "Jesus, I ask You, give me the strength for battle. Let it be done to me according to Your most holy will. My soul is enamored of Your most holy will." (*Diary*, 1498)

This passage from St. Faustina's *Diary* is very similar to the beautiful Psalm 77:

> In the day of my trouble I seek the Lord;
> in the night my hand is stretched out without wearying;
> my soul refuses to be comforted.
> I think of God, and I moan;
> I meditate, and my spirit faints. (vv. 2–3)

As 1 Corinthians 10:13 tells us: "God is faithful, and he will not let you be tempted beyond your strength, but with the temptation will also provide the way of escape, that you may be able to endure it." Faith tells us that this applies, too, to issues, dependencies, and addictions: We will not be tempted beyond our strength. Echoing this, Our Lord gives five points of advice to St. Faustina:

> First, do not fight against a temptation by yourself, but disclose it to the confessor at once, and then the temptation will lose all its force. Second, during these ordeals do not lose your peace; live in My presence; ask My Mother and the Saints for help. Third, have the certitude that I am looking at you and supporting you. Fourth, do not fear either struggles of the soul or any temptations, because I am supporting you; if only you are willing to fight, know that the victory is always on your side. Fifth, know that by fighting bravely you give Me great glory and amass merits for yourself. Temptation gives you a chance to show Me your fidelity" (*Diary*, 1560).

From a pastoral perspective, Our Lord's directives to St. Faustina provide great hope. God calls us to Himself through His Son, in the Holy Spirit, through the sacramental life and thus through the Sacred Liturgy and divine worship. We need to turn to the sacraments, especially Confession, and be drawn closer to our God. We mustn't let Satan stand in our way. Whatever our issues, dependencies, or even addictions, we can manage and overcome them through God's grace.

Virtue and Vice

Any discussion of issues, dependencies, and addictions necessarily relates to virtue and vice. Psalm 1 gives us a glimpse of this truth:

> Blessed is the man who does not walk
>   in the counsel of the wicked,
> Nor stand in the way of sinners,
>   nor sit in company with scoffers.
> Rather, the law of the LORD is his joy;
>   and on his law he meditates day and night.
> He is like a tree
>   planted near streams of water,
>   that yields its fruit in season;
> Its leaves never wither;
>   whatever he does prospers.
> But not so are the wicked, not so! (vv. 1–4)

The section of the *Catechism* about virtue opens at number 1803 with Philippians 4:8:

> Whatever is true, whatever is honorable, whatever is just, whatever is pure, whatever is lovely, whatever is gracious, if there is any excellence, if there is anything worthy of praise, think about these things.

The *Catechism* continues:

> A virtue is a habitual and firm disposition to do the good. It allows the person not only to perform good acts, but to give the best of himself. The virtuous person tends toward the

> good with all his sensory and spiritual powers; he pursues the good and chooses it in concrete actions. "The goal of a virtuous life is to become like God."[40] (1803)

Wow! The goal of a virtuous life is to become like God. (Thank you, St. Gregory of Nyssa!) I love it that our one, holy, catholic, and apostolic faith can be so simple and straightforward. This, then, is the definition of a virtue, which we develop by cooperating with the grace of God, the First (or Primary) Mover. Through sanctifying grace given to us in the seven sacraments, we become participators in the divine life of God; that is, we "become partakers of the divine nature" (2 Pet. 1:4). That's not a metaphor! Based on Scripture and Sacred Tradition, we know that through grace we can enter into communion with God here on earth. Maybe this is why St. Paul, in his First Letter to Timothy, states: "Aim at righteousness, godliness, faith, love, steadfastness, gentleness" (6:11). And St. Isidore of Seville tells us that we benefit from our friendships with others who practice the same virtuous traits: "Seek the association of persons who are good. For if you are the companion of their life, you will also be the companion of their virtue."[41]

As the *Catechism*'s definition of virtue tells us, we are to tend toward the good and the true and choose them with all of our *sensory powers* (that is, the five senses of sight, smell, taste, touch, and hearing) and *spiritual powers* (that is, the faculties of the soul: intellect, will, memory, and imagination). St. Alphonsus Liguori sums it all up this way:

> [God gave man] a soul, made in His likeness, and endowed with memory, intellect and will; He gave him a body equipped

[40] St. Gregory of Nyssa, *De beatitudinibus*.

[41] Quoted in Fr. Charles Fehrenbach, *Every Day Is Gift* (Totowa, NJ: Catholic Book Publishing, 1984), 53.

> with the senses; it was for him that He created Heaven and earth and such an abundance of things. He made all these things out of love for man, so that all creation might serve man, and man in turn might love God out of gratitude for so many gifts.[42]

Illustrating the beauty of this teaching, St. John Bosco provides an important lesson concerning the abuse of the sense of sight. He warns, "Guard your eyes, since they are the windows through which sin enters the soul."[43]

Now, for a list of some core virtues, we look to the *Catechism* (1803–1832), which gives us these categories: the cardinal virtues, the theological virtues, and the gifts and fruits of the Holy Spirit. The cardinal virtues are prudence, justice, fortitude, and temperance. The word "cardinal" comes from the Latin *cardinalis*, meaning "hinge" (such as the hinge on which a door hangs). In other words, the whole of the moral life "hinges" on these four virtues.

> Four virtues play a pivotal role and accordingly are called "cardinal"; all the others are grouped around them. They are: prudence, justice, fortitude, and temperance. "If anyone loves righteousness, [Wisdom's] labors are virtues; for she teaches temperance and prudence, justice, and courage" (Wisd. 8:7). These virtues are praised under other names in many passages of Scripture. (CCC 1805)

Regarding the theological virtues, the *Catechism* states:

> The theological virtues are the foundation of Christian moral activity; they animate it and give it its special character. They inform and give life to all the moral virtues.

[42] *Tract. De praxi amandi Iesum Christum edit. Latina* (Rome, 1909).
[43] Quoted in Thigpen, *Dictionary of Quotes*, 262.

> They are infused by God into the souls of the faithful to make them capable of acting as his children and of meriting eternal life. They are the pledge of the presence and action of the Holy Spirit in the faculties of the human being. There are three theological virtues: faith, hope, and charity (cf. 1 Cor. 13:13). (1813)

The seven gifts of the Holy Spirit are "permanent dispositions which make man docile in following the promptings of the Holy Spirit" (CCC 1830). They can also be considered virtues, and they are: wisdom, understanding, counsel, fortitude, knowledge, piety, and fear of the Lord. "They belong in their fullness to Christ.... They complete and perfect the virtues of those who receive them. They make the faithful docile in readily obeying divine inspiration" (CCC 1831). That is why the gifts of the Holy Spirit play such a strong and important role in a life of virtue and holiness.

Then there are twelve fruits of the Holy Spirit, described in paragraph 1832 of the *Catechism*, which can also double as virtues in a life well-lived: charity, joy, peace, patience, kindness, goodness, generosity, gentleness, faithfulness, modesty, self-control, and chastity.

The possession and practice of the gifts and fruits of the Holy Spirit are conveyed well in these two passages from Scripture:

> Let your good spirit lead me on a level path. (Ps. 143:10, quoted in CCC 1831)

> For all who are led by the Spirit of God are sons of God.... If children, then heirs, heirs of God and fellow heirs with Christ. (Rom. 8:14, 17, quoted in CCC 1831)

In short, the life of virtue is about integrity and consistency. We can see this in three apt selections from Scripture—specifically Paul's letters—all of which contain the word "whatever," indicating that Christ should imbue *all aspects* of our lives, body and soul:

> Let no one seek his own good, but the good of his neighbor.... So, whether you eat or drink, or *whatever you do*, do all to the glory of God. (1 Cor. 10:24, 31; emphasis added)
>
> And *whatever you do*, in word or deed, *do everything* in the name of the Lord Jesus, giving thanks to God the Father through him. (Col. 3:17; emphasis added)
>
> *Whatever your task*, work heartily, as serving the Lord and not men, knowing that from the Lord you will receive the inheritance as your reward; you are serving the Lord Christ. (Col. 3:23–24; emphasis added)

Growth in personal holiness by way of virtue comes from the Father, through the Son, and in the Holy Spirit—in *whatever* we do. This is why it's important to try to live a strong Trinitarian spirituality: offering everything throughout our day (prayer, work, recreation, and our associations with others) *to* the Father, *through* the Son, *in* the Holy Spirit. For example, the first thing you can do when you get up is pray a Morning Offering, a staple in Catholic spirituality. And, as mentioned earlier, at midday, you can perform a short examination of conscience (called the *particular examen*), focusing on a particular vice you are trying to root out or a particular virtue you are trying to nurture. And then, at the end of the day, you can perform a general examination of conscience (called the *general examen*), wherein you look with clear eyes at your conduct throughout the whole day. Both of these short examinations—which should take only a few minutes each—you can complete with an Act of Contrition (see appendix A).

Luke 6:38 tells us something about the effort we put into our growth in virtue: "For the measure you give will be the measure you get back." Jesus indicates throughout the Gospel, but especially in this discourse, that our future fortunes, in terms of our relationship with Him, are up to us. Our actions boomerang, for good or for ill, as the following Scripture passages attest:

> Judge not, and you will not be judged; condemn not, and you will not be condemned; forgive, and you will be forgiven; give, and it will be given to you. (Luke 6:37–38)
>
> As you wish that men would do to you, do so to them. (Luke 6:31)
>
> For judgment is without mercy to one who has shown no mercy. (James 2:13)
>
> God is not mocked, for whatever a man sows, that he will also reap. (Gal. 6:7)
>
> He who sows sparingly will also reap sparingly, and he who sows bountifully will also reap bountifully. (2 Cor. 9:6)

God has granted us an amazing but challenging freedom to determine our own earthly and eternal destinies by our choices. We are to cooperate with God, the Primary Mover, as an active instrument of His will, in His grace, moving toward holiness. Understanding this, how can we hold that unforgiving grudge—like the decades-long silent treatment over a Thanksgiving Day slight we discussed earlier? Indeed, we are called to so much more. So, be a grown-up Christian. Own it. Get over it. As 1 Thessalonians 4:3 states, it is God's will that you grow in holiness. And let us remember that each action and reaction can have multiple ramifications. Let's recall the four consequences of sin from our first chapter: personal, social, ecclesial and cosmic. Through sin, we disrupt our relationships with ourselves, with others, with Christ, and with all of creation.

St. Ambrose sums up our lesson on virtue by stating: "Virtue is a very wonderful thing for us. It is the good of life; the fruit of a clear conscience, and the peace of the innocent."[44]

Vice, on the other hand, is "a habit acquired by repeated sin and violation of the proper norms of human morality."[45] We can think of them in terms of their opposing virtues, or in terms of the "capital sins," from which all other sins flow. These are: pride, avarice (greed), envy, wrath (anger), lust, gluttony, and sloth. Sin, as we've said, creates a proclivity to sin.

> It engenders vice by repetition of the same acts. This results in perverse inclinations which cloud conscience and corrupt the concrete judgment of good and evil. Thus sin tends to reproduce itself and reinforce itself, but it cannot destroy the moral sense at its root. (CCC 1865)

That last sentence is so important: Indeed, we can always come back to God's grace at His constant invitation through our free will. In short, we are free and are meant to live free. But as 1 Peter 2:16 states so well: "Live as free men, yet without using your freedom as a pretext for evil; but live as servants of God." And St. Augustine warns us what happens if we do otherwise: "If we choose to be sick once again [that is, by falling into further sin], we will not only harm ourselves, but show ingratitude to the [Divine] Physician as well."[46]

Summing up vice, then, St. Basil the Great states simply, "The definition of vice is as follows: It is the wrong use—in violation of the Lord's command—of what has been given us by God for a good purpose."[47] Exhorting us to root out vice and pursue virtue,

[44] Quoted in Fehrenbach, *Every Day Is Gift*, 181.

[45] CCC, glossary, s.v. "vice"; cf. no. 1866.

[46] Sermon 23A.

[47] Quoted in Fehrenbach, *Every Day Is Gift*, 30.

Proverbs 15:9 tells us: "The way of the wicked is an abomination to the Lord, but he loves him who pursues righteousness." And 3 John 1:11 states, "Beloved, do not imitate evil but imitate good. He who does good is of God; he who does evil has not seen God."

Now let's look not only at the seven capital sins but also at their opposite corresponding virtues and their opposite extremes:

Capital Sin (Laxity)	Opposite Corresponding Virtue (Balance)	Opposite Extreme (Rigidity)
Pride	Humility	Self-loathing
Avarice (Greed)	Generosity	Wastefulness
Lust	Chastity	Prudishness
Anger	Meekness (Patience)	Servility
Gluttony	Temperance	Deficiency
Envy	Kindness (Brotherly Love)	Pusillanimity (Cowardice/Timidity)
Sloth (Acedia)	Diligence	Workaholism

It's important to remember that each of the seven capital sins has not only an opposite virtue to counteract it, but also an opposite extreme that, though antithetical to it, can do *just as much damage* in a person's life. Consider sloth and workaholism, which, though opposites, both take us away from the virtuous mean—one by neglecting our work duties, another by focusing so extremely on our work duties that we neglect other duties. Regardless which of these a person suffers from, diligence is the virtue that needs to be practiced to overcome it. St. Elizabeth Ann Seton reminds us of something very important here: "Our dear Savior was never in extremes.... We know certainly that our God calls us to a holy life, that He gives us every grace, every abundant grace; and though we are so weak of ourselves, this grace is able to carry us through every obstacle and difficulty."[48]

A quick point about habitual sins that often emerge from capital sins or from their opposite extremes, or both: Genuine repentance and confession of a habitual sin in the Sacrament of Confession does restore grace to the soul, but the *removal* of an *ingrained disposition to sin*—that is, a vice—will often require a great deal of effort and self-denial on the penitent's part until the contrary virtue is finally acquired.[49] In other words, taking our bad habits to the Sacrament of Confession will result in forgiveness and help begin the healing process, but the words of absolution from the priest *do not* function as a magic wand that roots out the vices that impact our everyday lives. That's *not* how Confession works—though it is an essential first step. To root out an ingrained disposition in your personhood will take much effort and practice of the opposite virtue as required by God's grace.

This is why our discussion of virtue and vice is connected with issues, dependencies, and addictions. Every vice can be sorted into one of these categories: Every vice burrows into your psyche and makes you feel as if it wouldn't be worth it to give it up—or, worse, as if you can't live without it—like an addiction. This is what the *Catechism* means when it says that sin creates a further disposition (proclivity) to sin (see CCC 1865).

[48] From a conference to her spiritual daughters.

[49] See CCC, glossary, s.v. "vice"; cf. no. 1866.

We break free of this cycle through genuine hope in God's grace. And that hope really is confidence: *con fide*, "with faith." Hope (again, one of the three theological virtues) is how we can rejoice even in adversity and consider it a privilege to suffer for Jesus' sake. "In hope we are saved" (Rom. 8:24). Contrary to the common saying, hope *does not* spring eternal in the human heart. It must be given by God. As stated earlier, hope is an infused theological virtue. Lasting hope is divinely possible through a life of grace. Here are some Scripture passages that convey this truth beautifully:

> Blessed be the God and Father of our Lord Jesus Christ! By his great mercy we have been born anew to a living hope through the resurrection of Jesus Christ from the dead. (1 Pet. 1:3)

> [May] the God of our Lord Jesus Christ, the Father of glory, . . . give you a spirit of wisdom and of revelation in the knowledge of him, having the eyes of your hearts enlightened, that you may know what is the hope to which he has called you. (Eph. 1:17–18)

> Hope does not disappoint us, because God's love has been poured into our hearts through the Holy Spirit who has been given to us. (Rom. 5:5)

> May the God of hope fill you with all joy and peace in believing, so that by the power of the Holy Spirit you may abound in hope. (Rom. 15:13)

Through this hope—including confidence in Christ's forgiveness—we can be confirmed in our growth in virtue:

> For the sake of eternal life, my brothers, let us do the will of the Father Who called us, resisting the temptations that lead us into sin and striving earnestly to advance in virtue. . . .

> We should blot out past sins by being truly sorry for them, and then we shall be saved.[50]

God is always there to help us to overcome vice and to advance in virtue. As Psalm 17 gloriously proclaims: "For thou lightest my lamp, O Lord: O my God, enlighten my darkness. For by thee I shall be delivered from temptation; and through my God I shall go over a wall" (29–30, Douay-Rheims).[51]

The Importance of Self-Knowledge

After all this discussion about issues, dependencies and addictions, and growth in virtue and the shunning of vice, it should be obvious that one of the first steps in growing in Christian holiness is *self-knowledge*. The phrase "Know thyself" was well known even among the ancient Greek philosophers such as Socrates and Plato. In other words, we must know and admit our virtues in order to advance them, and similarly, we must know and admit our vices in order to begin to uproot them out of our lives. For example, aren't we exhorted to make a good examination of conscience before going to Confession? (See CCC 1454.) That is self-knowledge.

This isn't just my insight: It comes directly from the Angelic Doctor, St. Thomas Aquinas. The only way we can move toward the Lord is by being conscious of and realistic about the things that will sink us—beginning with our vices, our issues, our dependencies, our addictions: pride, selfishness, anger, lust, envy, greed, cowardice, and so on. Here are some fantastic quotes from the saints that convey the vital importance of self-knowledge in the spiritual life:

[50] From a second-century homily attributed to pseudo-Clement of Rome.

[51] Psalm 18:28–29 in other translations.

St. Dorotheus, Abbot: "The reason for all disturbance, if we look to its roots, is that no one finds fault with himself. This is the source of all annoyance and distress."[52]

St. Dorotheus, Abbot: "The man who finds fault with himself accepts all things cheerfully—misfortune, loss, disgrace, dishonor, and any other kind of adversity. He believes that he is deserving of all these things, and nothing can disturb him. No one could be more at peace than this man."[53]

St. Augustine: "A man cannot hope to find God unless he first finds himself."[54]

St. Peter of Alcántara: "We all talk of reforming others without ever reforming ourselves."[55]

St. Francis de Sales: "Have patience with all things, but chiefly have patience with yourself. Do not lose courage in considering your own imperfections, but instantly set about remedying them—every day begin the task anew."[56]

St. Augustine: "I will confess, therefore, what I know of myself, and also what I do not know. The knowledge that I have of myself, I possess because You have enlightened me; while the knowledge of myself that I do not yet possess will

[52] Doct. 7, *De accusation sui ipsius*, 1–2: PG 88, 1695–1699.

[53] Doct. 13, *De accusation sui ipsius*, 2–3: PG 88, 1699.

[54] *Confessions*, bk. 3, chap. 4.

[55] Quoted in Fr. Alban Butler, *Lives of the Saints*, vol. 10, *October* (Collegeville, MN: Liturgical Press, 1996), 136.

[56] The original source of this popular quotation is unclear, but it appears in the nineteenth-century text *The Beauties of St. Francis de Sales*.

not be mine until my darkness shall be made as the noonday sun before Your face."[57]

St. Albert the Great: "To ascend to God means nothing else than to enter into oneself. And, indeed, he who enters into the secret place of his own soul passes beyond himself, and does in very truth, ascend to God."[58]

St. Hippolytus: "The saying 'Know yourself' means therefore that we should recognize and acknowledge in ourselves the God Who made us in His own image, for if we do this, we in turn will be recognized and acknowledged by our Maker."[59]

Many saints have taught that the person of true sanctity is the one who is equally aware of his dark side as he is of his need for the grace and mercy of God. Why is this? Because if all one does is focus on one's sins and failings, this can lead to the sin of *despair*. On the other hand, if all one does is focus on God's mercy and love while making no real effort to overcome one's sins and vices, then this can lead to the sin of *presumption*. In short, we do not want to despair of God's mercy, nor do we want to presume on His mercy. Maybe this why it is said that St. Philip Neri, upon waking each morning, would pray this Morning Offering: "Watch me, O Lord, this day; for, abandoned to myself, I shall surely betray Thee."[60]

St. Augustine exhorts us always to move forward, but we need the self-knowledge to see what we are growing *in* and *toward*:

[57] *Confessions*, bk. 10, chap. 7.

[58] *On Union with God*, chap. 7.

[59] *On the Refutation of All Heresies*, bk. 10, chap. 30: PG 16, 3452–3453.

[60] *St. Vincent's Manual: Containing a Selection of Prayers and Devotional Exercises*, originally published by the Sisters of Charity of St. Vincent de Paul in 1856.

> Keep on making progress. This progress, however, must be in virtue; for there are some, the Apostle warns, whose only progress is in vice. If you make progress, you will be continuing your journey, but be sure that your progress is in virtue, true faith, and right living.[61]

And St. Catherine of Siena recorded in her *Dialogue* these words of God speaking to her:

> Never go outside the knowledge of yourself, and, by humbling yourself in the valley of humility, you will know Me and yourself, from which knowledge you will draw all that is necessary.... In self-knowledge, then, you will humble yourself, seeing that, in yourself, you do not even exist; for your very being, as you will learn, is derived from Me.

In other words, self-knowledge is the first step needed to be drawn into the divine love and divine communion that the Almighty and Trinitarian God desires for us with Him—all things *to* the Father, *through* the Son, *in* the Holy Spirit. Make your daily life Trinitarian. Whether during the Sacred Liturgy on Sunday or a weekday, at home with your family, at work, or even while at the mall, all things should lead to a greater love of the Blessed Trinity. God knows us, and He wants us to know Him. And a big part of that knowing is gained through self-knowledge in everyday activities, all the while knowing in Whose image and likeness we are made (see Gen. 1:26–27).

Further illustrating these truths, St. Catherine of Siena also recorded these words of God in her *Dialogue*:

> In knowing yourself, you will come to know better the overflowing generosity of My charity. But if you make no effort

[61] *Sermo* 256, 1.3.4; *PL* 38, 1191–1193.

> to know yourself, you won't know Me. [And] because you don't know Me, you won't love Me. And because you don't love Me, you won't serve Me.[62]

Pope St. Gregory the Great, too, provides another great lesson on the importance of self-knowledge and how it reciprocates God's love for us. This lesson regards Mary Magdalene being the first person to meet Our Risen Lord at the tomb on Easter Morning:

> *Jesus says to her: Mary.* Jesus is not recognized when He calls her "woman"; so He calls her by name, as though He were saying: "Recognize Me as I recognize you; for I do not know you as I know others; I know you as yourself." And so Mary, once addressed by name, recognizes Who is speaking. She immediately calls Him *rabboni*, that is to say, *teacher*, because the one Whom she sought outwardly was the one Who inwardly taught her to keep on searching.[63]

To acknowledge the intimacy that Jesus wants to have with us in our spiritual growth, we must draw ever closer to Him. As St. Paul tells us: "Let us conduct ourselves becomingly as in the day, not in reveling and drunkenness, not in debauchery and licentiousness, not in quarreling and jealousy. But put on the Lord Jesus Christ" (Rom. 13:13–14).

But it is self-love that most often prevents us from growing in self-knowledge. Yet, it's good to be reminded that, as Rev. Augustine DiNoia, O.P., states: "Dying to self is not fatal."[64] In fact, dying to self will enable you to live your life more fully. This is why St.

[62] Quoted in *Magnificat* 20, no. 4 (June 2018): 170.

[63] Homily 25.

[64] Quoted in Craig Steven Titus, ed., *On Wings of Faith and Reason: The Christian Difference in Culture and Science* (Arlington, VA: Institute for the Psychological Sciences Press, 2008), 125.

Dominic famously said that "a person who governs his passions is master of the world."[65]

A lack of self-knowledge—and an excess of self-love—manifests itself in disorder of the soul. Thomas à Kempis teaches in *The Imitation of Christ*, "A man who lives at peace suspects no one, but a man who is tense and agitated by evil is troubled with all kinds of suspicions. He is never even at peace with himself, nor does he permit others to be at peace."[66] Elsewhere in *The Imitation of Christ*, we read something very similar regarding the importance of self-knowledge: "Persons who would be truly spiritual ... must especially beware of themselves, for in overcoming themselves, they will the more easily subdue all things else. The most noble and perfect victory is the triumph over oneself."[67] And in James 3 we read, "For where jealousy and selfish ambition exist, there will be disorder and every vile practice. But the wisdom from above is first pure, then peaceable, gentle, open to reason, full of mercy and good fruits, without uncertainty or insincerity" (16–17).

That "wisdom from above" comes from communion with our Trinitarian God, living a life of His sanctifying grace. Here's how the Apostle James put it in an earlier part of his letter:

> Blessed is the man who endures trial, for when he has stood the test he will receive the crown of life which God has promised to those who love him. Let no one say when he is tempted, "I am tempted by God"; for God cannot be tempted with evil and he himself tempts no one; but each person is tempted when he is lured and enticed by his own desire. Then

[65] Quoted in Bert Ghezzi, ed., *Mystics and Miracles: True Stories of Lives Touched by God* (Chicago: Loyola Press, 2004), 94.

[66] Bk. 2, chap. 3.

[67] Bk. 3, chap. 53.

desire when it has conceived gives birth to sin; and sin when it is full-grown brings forth death. (1:12–15)

That death is the result of mortal sin, which arises once we have become acclimated to smaller, venial sins and habitual vices. So, in the moral life, we need to be vigilant and watchful of self. As St. Francis of Assisi says, "Above all the grace and the gifts that Christ gives to His beloved is that of overcoming self"[68]—that is, overcoming the vices and sins to which our desires incline us. St. Teresa of Avila says, "To be humble is to walk in truth."[69] She means here that we recognize in an honest and realistic way the talents that we have and those that we lack (again, *self-knowledge!*); we accept what God has given us and are comfortable with ourselves. In this way, we become docile to the truth of Christ and His will for us. Humility makes us free—"detached," if you will.

The *freedom* of humility is related, then, to the *virtue* of humility. St. Thomas Aquinas teaches that detachment is loving persons, places, and things in the way God intends us to love them—that is, for their genuine goodness, which is always a reflection of His goodness. Detachment is "that virtue which frees an individual from any inordinate attachment to another person, place, object, or state of mind. True detachment is not simply a lack of care. Rather, it is a liberation from any excessive affection that would hinder one's love and worship of God."[70]

To achieve this detachment—this properly *ordered* love—we need to know (by way of self-knowledge) our weaknesses and control

[68] Quoted in Ron Rhodes, ed., *1001 Unforgettable Quotes about God, Faith, and the Bible* (Eugene, OR: Harvest House Publishers, 2011), 197.

[69] *Interior Castle*, Sixth Mansion, 10, 8.

[70] Fr. Peter Stravinskas, *Catholic Dictionary, Revised* (Huntington, IN: Our Sunday Visitor, 2002); cf. CCC 2544–2550.

our passions. It is important to note here that *passions*, *emotions*, and *feelings* (three terms used synonymously in the moral life) are *neutral* in and of themselves. They are neither good nor evil. Rather, to make a moral judgment about a passion, feeling, or emotion (for example, joy), we have to know what "end" or "object" it is directed toward. Is a man joyful because he knows he will be meeting his adulterous lover this evening? Or is he joyful because it's his twenty-third wedding anniversary, and he's looking forward to taking his wife out to dinner? The *Catechism* explains this moral principle well:

> In themselves passions are neither good nor evil. They are morally qualified only to the extent that they effectively engage reason and will. Passions are said to be voluntary, "either because they are commanded by the will or because the will does not place obstacles in their way."[71] It belongs to the perfection of the moral or human good that the passions be governed by reason.[72]
>
> Strong feelings are not decisive for the morality or the holiness of persons; they are simply the inexhaustible reservoir of images and affections in which the moral life is expressed. Passions are morally good when they contribute to a good action, evil in the opposite case. The upright will orders the movements of the senses it appropriates to the good and to beatitude; an evil will succumbs to disordered passions and exacerbates them. Emotions and feelings can be taken up into the virtues or perverted by the *vices*. (1767–1768)

So, self-indulgence and compulsive behaviors are not expressions of authentic human freedom, as the modern-day relativist and secularist culture would have us believe.

[71] St. Thomas Aquinas, *Summa Theologica*, I-II, q. 24, art. 1.
[72] Cf. St. Thomas Aquinas, *Summa Theologica*, I-II, q. 24, art. 3.

> Therefore gird up your minds, be sober, set your hope fully upon the grace that is coming to you at the revelation of Jesus Christ. As obedient children, do not be conformed to the passions of your former ignorance. (1 Pet. 1:13–14)

Detachment, in its truest sense, then, is really about loving persons, places, and things *the way God intends us to love them*; that is, in an *ordinate* way as opposed to an *inordinate* way. Illustrating this, *The Imitation of Christ* states, "No matter how little it is, anything loved and regarded inordinately will keep you back from the supreme Good and corrupt your soul."[73] So, detachment, in its authentic sense, protects us from establishing "inordinate attachments" to persons, places, and things. And so it is, too, that detachment does not negate the existence of love. In fact, detachment is precisely about loving things *properly*, in an ordered sense. Indeed, such proper love can lead one to "strive diligently for perfect interior freedom and self-mastery in every place, in every action and occupation, so that you be not the slave of anything, but that all things be under your control."[74]

As we close this chapter on virtue and vice and the importance of self-knowledge, St. Peter exhorts us to remember that God wills that, through a life of His sanctifying grace working in us, we become partakers of the divine nature:

> His divine power has granted to us all things that pertain to life and godliness, through the knowledge of him who called us to his own glory and excellence, by which he has granted to us his precious and very great promises, that through these you may escape from the corruption that is in the world because of passion, and become partakers of

[73] Bk. 3, chap. 42.

[74] Bk. 3, chap. 38.

> the divine nature. For this very reason make every effort to supplement your faith with virtue, and virtue with knowledge, and knowledge with self-control, and self-control with steadfastness, and steadfastness with godliness, and godliness with brotherly affection, and brotherly affection with love. For if these things are yours and abound, they keep you from being ineffective or unfruitful in the knowledge of our Lord Jesus Christ. For whoever lacks these things is blind and shortsighted and has forgotten that he was cleansed from his old sins. (2 Pet. 1:3–9).

This sharing in the divine nature through God's sanctifying grace is made manifest at each and every Mass. In fact, during the Offertory Rite, while the priest mixes a bit of water with the wine (prior to the Consecration), he prays specifically that we may "come to share in the divinity of Christ." This mixing of water and wine is symbolic of the two natures of Christ, human and divine, united in one Divine Person: the Second Person of the Trinity. The two natures of Christ come to us in the Eucharist, just as they did in His Sacred Incarnation. Let us heed the great call to partake in this great gift through God's sanctifying grace offered in the Eucharist.

Now that we have a greater awareness of vice and virtue and understand the need for possessing good self-knowledge so as to advance in God's sanctifying grace, let us discuss the Sacrament of Penance and Reconciliation—holy Confession.

Chapter 3

The Sacrament of Penance and Reconciliation

Thou hast held back my life from the
pit of destruction, for thou hast cast
all my sins behind thy back.

—Isaiah 38:17

Write this for the benefit of distressed souls: when a soul sees and realizes the gravity of its sins, when the whole abyss of the misery into which it immersed itself is displayed before its eyes, let it not despair, but with trust let it throw itself into the arms of My mercy, as a child into the arms of its beloved mother. These souls have a right of priority to My compassionate heart, they have first access to My mercy. Tell them that no soul that has called upon My mercy has been disappointed or brought to shame. I delight particularly in a soul which has placed its trust in My goodness.

—Our Lord to St. Faustina Kowalska (*Diary*, 1541)

Remedies to Sin: Conviction, Repentance, Forgiveness, and Mercy

"To the eyes of faith, no evil is greater than sin and nothing has worse consequences for sinners themselves, for the Church, and for the whole world" (CCC 1488). Thus speaks the *Catechism of the Catholic Church*, in no uncertain terms, about the reality and gravity of sin. Maybe this is why 1 Corinthians 15:34 tells us quite plainly: "Come to your right mind, and sin no more." If we consistently and unrepentantly fail to do the Father's will, Jesus will solemnly declare to us, as He does in Matthew 7:23: "I never knew you; depart from me, you evildoers."

If we don't listen and respond to God's word, our lives will collapse into ruin; even if we accumulate earthly success and pleasures, our souls will be in tatters. Thus, James 1:22 tells us, "But be doers of the word, and not hearers only, deceiving yourselves." The consequences of ignoring the Lord, as described in Scripture, are stark: 2 Kings 24 describes the beginning of the Babylonian Captivity of the Jews, in response to their faithlessness; Romans 6:16 describes slavery and death as the wages of sin; throughout 1 John 2, the Apostle writes of spiritual blindness to God and His goodness as a consequence of sin; and, of course, in the Gospels, such as in the "resurrection of judgment" described in John 5:29, we are taught that Hell awaits those who reject the Lord.

In addition, and even worse, by sinning we continue to crucify Our Lord and Savior Jesus Christ. The writer of Hebrews says of those who leave God's friendship that "they crucify the Son of God on their own account and hold him up to contempt" (6:6). And in 1 Corinthians 1:17, Paul implies that when we reject the gospel we allow "the cross of Christ [to] be emptied of its power."

This is the reality of sin, and we must look at it honestly. But it is also *not* the last word. St. Faustina recorded many words of comfort from the Lord in her *Diary*. Perhaps foremost among them is His description of the Sacrament of Confession as His Tribunal of Mercy:

> Pray for souls that they be not afraid to approach the tribunal of My mercy. Do not grow weary of praying for sinners. You know what a burden their souls are to My Heart. Relieve My deathly sorrow; dispense My mercy. (975)

And it's worth recalling this important passage from St. Faustina's *Diary*, mentioned in our first chapter:

> Write, speak of My mercy. Tell souls where they are to look for solace; that is, in the Tribunal of Mercy [the Sacrament of Reconciliation]. There the greatest miracles take place and are incessantly repeated. To avail oneself of this miracle, it is not necessary to go on a great pilgrimage or to carry out some external ceremony. It suffices to come with faith to the feet of My representative and to reveal to him one's misery, and the miracle of Divine Mercy will be fully demonstrated. Were a soul like a decaying corpse so that from a human standpoint, there would be no [hope of] restoration and everything would already seem to be lost. It is not so with God. The miracle of Divine Mercy restores that soul in full. Oh, how miserable are those who do not take advantage of the miracle of God's mercy. You will call out in vain, but it will be too late. (1448)

Now, it's very interesting that Our Lord refers to the Sacrament of Confession as a "Tribunal of Mercy." Why? Because a tribunal is a court (think, for example, of a marriage tribunal in a diocese, which has the task of judging marriage cases). So, Jesus is calling Confession a "court of mercy." And in first-century Jerusalem, who was the tribune? He was the one charged by the Romans to defend the accused party free of charge—what we would consider today a public defender.

How awesome is that! In the Sacrament of Confession, Jesus is your tribune, your public defender—free of charge—before the Just Judge, our Heavenly Father. And may we place the Holy Spirit in the jury box as just juror?

St. Faustina clearly absorbs Our Lord's description of the Sacrament of Confession as a "Tribunal of Mercy." Twice in her *Diary* she herself mentions this description of the sacrament. First, when she writes of a conversation between the Merciful God and a Sinful Soul, she has the soul saying these words:

> You have conquered, O Lord, my stony heart with Your goodness. In trust and humility I approach the tribunal of Your mercy, where You yourself absolve me by the hand of your representative. O Lord, I feel Your grace and Your peace filling my poor soul. I feel overwhelmed by Your mercy, O Lord. You forgive me, which is more than I dared to hope for or could imagine. Your goodness surpasses all my desires. And now, filled with gratitude for so many graces, I invite You to my heart. I wandered, like a prodigal child gone astray; but you did not cease to be my Father. Increase Your mercy toward me, for You see how weak I am. (1485)

Second, in a conversation between the Merciful God and a Perfect Soul, St. Faustina has the soul confidently saying these words regarding the Tribunal of Mercy:

> You have covered me with the cloak of Your mercy, pardoning my sins. Not once did You refuse Your pardon; You always had pity on me, giving me a new life of grace. To prevent doubts, You have entrusted me to the loving care of Your Church, that tender mother, who in Your name assures me of the truths of faith and watches lest I wander. Especially in the tribunal of Your mercy does my soul meet an ocean of favors. (1489)

This emphasis on mercy is not some new teaching or new reality of God; we see it throughout the Old Testament. For example, in the very first chapter of the book of the prophet Isaiah, we hear these words of the Lord:

> Wash yourselves; make yourselves clean; remove the evil of your doings from before my eyes; cease to do evil, learn to do good; seek justice, correct oppression;... though your sins are like scarlet, they shall be as white as snow; though they are red like crimson, they shall become like wool. (1:16–18)

And the prophet Jeremiah says:

> Return, faithless Israel, says the LORD. I will not look on you in anger, for I am merciful, says the LORD; I will not be angry for ever. Only acknowledge your guilt, that you rebelled against the LORD your God ... and that you have not obeyed my voice, says the LORD.... Return, O faithless children. (3:12–14)

In the New Testament, we could go on and on: James 5:16 ("Therefore confess your sins to one another, and pray for one another, that you may be healed"); Matthew 9:13 ("I desire mercy, and not sacrifice"); Ephesians 2:4 ("God ... is rich in mercy"). The Scriptural record is clear: Our God is merciful, but we must be convicted, forthright, and contrite about the ways we have offended Him. This is where the Tribunal of Mercy—the Sacrament of Confession—comes in.

During my priestly ministry, I have discerned several reasons why people hesitate to approach the Sacrament of Confession. Here are five of the most common:

- † *Fear*: Though the vast majority of priests are kind and understanding confessors, many potential penitents fear being judged or scolded.
- † *Pride*: Confessing sins means confronting that we've genuinely done wrong and need God's help to heal. Our personal pride rebels against this.
- † *Shame*: Though a well-ordered guilt should impel us to the Sacrament of Confession, shame can keep us away because of the realization that we have to admit our sins to another—and speaking our sins out loud feels unbearable.
- † *Ignorance*: This is twofold. First, we can be ignorant of the reality of sin in our lives and its devastating consequences if it goes unchecked. Second, we can be ignorant of the necessity of sacramental Confession for the forgiveness of mortal sins.
- † *Unavailability*: Too often there simply aren't enough times offered for Confession at local parishes, or there is no option for anonymity, which is the *right* of every penitent according to the Church's discipline of this sacrament.

A different kind of objection to the sacrament is the claim that we can and should go "straight to God" with our sins to have them forgiven. Well, you can do that for venial sins, but mortal sins require the Sacrament of Confession. Furthermore, did we go "straight to God" for our Baptism? Did we go "straight to God" for our Confirmation? Matrimony? The Anointing of the Sick or the other sacraments?

The truth—that Catholics usually understand in other contexts—is that the Church and Her ministers and sacraments mediate God's grace, and this is as God designed it. Consider the Old Testament, which is shot through with mediation in the form of the prophets, who bring God's saving message to the people. And in the New Testament, God sends the chief Mediator, the God-Man, Jesus Christ, as Savior of the world.

On how to approach Confession faithfully and confidently, St. Faustina tells us:

> As regards Holy confession . . . before I approach the confessional, I shall first enter the open and most merciful Heart of the Savior. When I leave the confessional, I shall rouse in my soul great gratitude to the Most Holy Trinity for this wonderful and inconceivable miracle of mercy that is wrought in my soul. And the more miserable my soul is, the more I feel the ocean of God's mercy engulfing me and giving me strength and great power. (*Diary*, 225)

Indeed, we should not be afraid to return again and again to the Tribunal of Mercy. Some of the following is a review from our first chapter, but it's worth repeating given that the Sacrament of Confession is closely related to growth in self-knowledge and a strong spiritual life.

Recall that the grace of the sacrament can protect us from sin by strengthening our resolve and reforming our habits. So, although we are required by Church law to go to Confession at least once a year if we are conscious of mortal sin, we still benefit from the time-honored tradition of going monthly (say, on First Friday in honor of the Sacred Heart of Jesus, or on First Saturday in honor of the Immaculate Heart of Mary). A faithful, monthly penitent most likely never, or at least infrequently, has mortal sin to confess, because the fervent practice of monthly Confession keeps him from committing mortal sin. And remember that Pope Pius XII recommended the practice of frequent Confession, even if only venial sins are in question:

> By it, genuine self-knowledge is increased, Christian humility grows, bad habits are corrected, spiritual neglect and tepidity are resisted, the conscience is purified, the will strengthened, a salutary self-control is attained, and grace is increased in virtue of the Sacrament itself.[75]

Here we see nine benefits of the sacrament, whether it be just venial sins or mortal sins, or a combination, that are confessed. Let's look briefly at each of these benefits:

† *Self-knowledge is increased.* As we discussed in Chapter 2, many saints make clear in their writing and teaching that self-knowledge is needed to grow in holiness. This means knowing and admitting your virtues so you can *advance them* in your life, and knowing and admitting your vices so you can *uproot them* out of your life.

† *Christian humility grows*. Humility is the "moral virtue that keeps a person from reaching beyond himself. It is the virtue that restrains the unruly desire for personal greatness and leads people to an orderly love of themselves based on a true appreciation of their position with respect to God and their neighbors."[76] Not only does the practice of frequent Confession help us to grow in humility, but the very act of making a good examination of conscience (required before even stepping into the confessional) is humbling—*and* it helps us to grow in self-knowledge.

[75] *Mystici Corporis Christi*, no. 88.

[76] Fr. John Hardon, *Modern Catholic Dictionary* (Bardstown, KY: Eternal Life Publications, 2000), 260.

- † *Bad habits are corrected.* Little by little, through frequent Confession and honesty with one's confessor, who will offer advice accordingly, bad habits *can* be overcome. Frequent, worthy reception of the Sacrament of Confession means frequent graces received from that sacrament for *those* bad habits.
- † *Spiritual neglect is resisted.* Let's say you are struggling to establish the practice of praying the daily Rosary or daily Chaplet of Divine Mercy, or even just making a Morning Offering upon rising each day. Your failures to practice these devotions would be examples of "spiritual neglects" that cause your spiritual life to suffer. Frequent Confession can help you get back on track, especially if your confessor assigns them to you as a penance and so you begin to carry them out more faithfully on your own.
- † *Spiritual tepidity is resisted.* Let's say you do, indeed, carry out such spiritual practices—but only infrequently. In other words, you carry them out in a tepid or lukewarm manner. The graces from frequent Confession can help ignite a renewed spiritual fervor that will help make your daily spiritual life grow stronger and more committed every day.
- † *Conscience is purified.* Confession of one's sins brings with it a purification and, importantly, peace of conscience. This is tied to the healing aspect of Confession. Indeed, Confession is one of two "healing" sacraments, along with the Sacrament of the Anointing of the Sick.
- † *The will is strengthened.* Whereas our intellect is what helps us "to know," our will is what helps us "to choose" (based on properly ordered love). Through the practice of frequent Confession, our wills become strengthened to help us more frequently choose good over evil, virtue over vice, and the beneficial over the malicious.

- † A *salutary self-control is achieved*. Only you can control you. Frequent Confession makes us simply want to "do better" in all aspects of daily living. It's the grace of the sacrament that propels us to control our lives better by practicing an *ordinate* love toward persons, places, and things and not an *inordinate*, or *disordered*, love toward them.
- † *Grace is increased in virtue of the sacrament itself*. Every sacrament, when it is received worthily, increases sanctifying grace in the soul. For Eucharist and Confession—the only two sacraments that can be received both repetitiously and frequently—this is especially true. In fact, the Sacrament of Confession can even help to perfect the grace of our Baptism. This is because Baptism, while wiping away the Original Sin we inherit from our first parents, also wipes away any personal sin (also called "actual sin") we might have (i.e., any venial or mortal sin). Confession always helps rid us of personal sin. We should add, though, that going to Confession out of scrupulosity is *not* helpful to the penitent, nor is it the intention of the sacrament. Scrupulosity is seeing sin where there is no sin at all but rather, say, a simple fault; or, seeing mortal sin when, in reality, it is a venial sin. Indeed, scruples can stunt one's growth in the spiritual life. Don't be your own savior; let Jesus Christ be your Savior.

God's Mercy: A Gift for the Asking

We've already established that sin doesn't have the last word, provided the person is convicted in his sin and responds to God's call to repentance and seeks forgiveness. This is where God's mercy helps to remedy the situation and bring about true healing. The section on "Mercy and Sin" in the *Catechism* begins with paragraphs 1846 and 1847:

> The Gospel is the revelation in Jesus Christ of God's mercy to sinners (cf. Luke 15). The angel announced to Joseph, "You shall call His name Jesus for He will save people from their sins" (Matt. 1:21). The same is true of the Eucharist, the sacrament of redemption: "This is my blood of the covenant, which is poured out for many for the forgiveness of sins" (Matt. 16:28). "God created us without us: but he did not will to save us without us."[77] To receive his mercy, we must admit our faults. "If we say we have no sin, we deceive ourselves, and the truth is not in us. If we confess our sins, he is faithful and just, and will forgive our sins and cleanse us from all unrighteousness" (1 John 1:8–9).

What great hope is given to the sinner through these words! God's mercy is always there for the asking. God seeks out sinners; He wants them to turn toward and return to Him. This is why He sent His Only-Begotten Son into the world, to help save a fallen world in need of redemption and salvation—all because of the reality of sin. In regard to the importance of our being "convicted" (or, convinced) of sin and of our need for repentance and forgiveness, and how the Holy Spirit aids in this process, the *Catechism* quotes John Paul II's *Dominum et vivificantem*:

> Conversion *requires convincing of sin*; it includes the interior judgment of conscience, and this, being a proof of the action of the Spirit of truth in man's inner most being, becomes at the same time the start of a new grant of grace and love: "Receive the Holy Spirit." Thus in this "convincing

[77] St. Augustine, *Sermo* 169.

> concerning sin" we discover *a double gift*: the gift of the truth of conscience and the gift of the certainty of redemption. The Spirit of truth is the Consoler. (CCC 1848)

The book of the prophet Ezekiel explains this conversion process well:

> But if a wicked man turns away from all his sins which he has committed and keeps all my statutes and does what is lawful and right, he shall surely live; he shall not die. None of the transgressions which he has committed shall be remembered against him; for the righteousness which he has done he shall live. (18:21–22)

This ties in nicely with our discussion of the importance and practice of virtue in the previous chapter. We can see, too, how conscience comes into play. Conscience is the "interior voice of a human being, within whose heart the inner law of God is inscribed. Moral conscience is a judgment of practical reason about the moral quality of a human action. It moves a person at the appropriate moment to do good and to avoid evil."[78] Illustrating this, Ezekiel further states:

> Therefore I will judge you, O house of Israel, every one according to his ways, says the LORD God. Repent and turn from all your transgressions, lest iniquity be your ruin. Cast away from you all the transgressions which you have committed against me, and get yourselves a new heart and a new spirit! . . . So turn, and live. (18:30–32)

Summing these truths up, the *Catechism* includes this beautiful meditation on Good Friday, the very day on which Our Lord and Savior Jesus Christ suffered and died for us:

[78] CCC, glossary, s.v. "conscience"; cf. nos. 1777, 1778, 1454.

> It is precisely in the Passion, when the mercy of Christ is about to vanquish it, that sin most clearly manifests its violence and its many forms: unbelief, murderous hatred, shunning and mockery by the leaders and the people, Pilate's cowardice and the cruelty of the soldiers, Judas' betrayal—so bitter to Jesus, Peter's denial and the disciples' flight. However, at the very hour of darkness, the hour of the prince of this world (cf. John 14:30), the sacrifice of Christ secretly becomes the source from which the forgiveness of our sins will pour forth inexhaustibly. (1851)

Pondering these great truths about the reality of sin and God's mercy, which *pours forth inexhaustibly* as a remedy for it, I can't help but think of the Divine Mercy image, with the two rays of blood and water flowing inexhaustibly from Christ's Sacred Heart. St. John Vianney said that "God's mercy is like an unleashed torrent. It bears away all hearts in its flood."[79]

Every time I read this quote, I think of a beautiful hiking trail in Connecticut that my fellow seminarians and I hiked during our priestly formation. One of the trails climbs and crests a beautiful mountain, and near the peak there is a waterfall. As the water crashes down, about forty-five feet below there is a rock formation that causes the waterfall to break into two streams. I have always thought it would be great to go up there at night with two floodlights, one red and one white, and put them at the base of the waterfall, shining upward. The mountainside would be turned into a representation of the Divine Mercy image, a meditation scene of the red and white rays flowing from the one source of the Sacred Heart of Jesus.

[79] Quoted in Johnston, *Voice of the Saints*, chap. 10.

In fact, precisely that imagery is used to describe Christ's merciful sacrifice in the First Letter of St. John: "This is He who came by water and blood, Jesus Christ, not with the water only but with the water and the blood" (5:6). The water, or white ray in the Divine Mercy image, symbolizes the cleansing power of Baptism, and the blood, or red ray, symbolizes the healing power of the sacrifice of the Eucharist. Taken together, they represent the mercy that is brought to fulfillment in a special way in the Sacrament of Confession.

Another important point worth mentioning here is that how we view Confession now, in this life, has a lot to say about how we view our Particular Judgment when we die. Here's the *Catechism* on how the Sacrament of Confession anticipates, in a real and certain way, the Particular Judgment that awaits each one of us at the time of our earthly death:

> In this sacrament, the sinner, placing himself before the merciful judgment of God, *anticipates* in a certain way *the judgment* to which he will be subjected at the end of his earthly life. For it is now, in this life, that we are offered the choice between life and death, and it is only by the road of conversion that we can enter the Kingdom, from which one is excluded by grave sin (cf. 1 Cor. 5:11; Gal. 5:19–21; Rev. 22:15). In converting to Christ through penance and faith, the sinner passes from death to life and "does not come into judgment" (John 5:24). (1470)

In other words, how we regard and treat Confession *now*, during this earthly life, says *a lot* about how we regard and treat our Particular Judgment—and, hence, the General Judgment, at which our Particular Judgment will be ratified. A nonchalant attitude toward Confession *now* both reveals and nurtures a nonchalant attitude toward the Last Things. On the other hand, faithfully approaching God's mercy *now* opens us to His mercy in the fullness of time. "In this is love perfected with us, that we may have confidence for the day of judgment" (1 John 4:17).

> "The whole power of the sacrament of Penance consists in restoring us to God's grace and joining us with Him in an intimate friendship."[80] Reconciliation with God is thus the purpose and effect of this sacrament. For those who receive the sacrament of Penance with contrite heart and religious disposition, "reconciliation is usually followed by peace and serenity of conscience with strong spiritual consolation."[81] Indeed, the sacrament of Reconciliation with God brings about a true "spiritual resurrection," restoration of the dignity and blessings of the life of the children of God, of which the most precious is friendship with God (cf. Luke 15:32). (CCC 1468)

Indeed, those who embrace and love the Sacrament of Confession now, approaching God's mercy with faithfulness and contrition, are converted to Christ right here and now. The sinner passes from death to life and so does not come into judgment. Scripture and tradition should give us confidence in this truth:

> "Return to me, says the LORD of hosts, and I will return to you.... Return from your evil ways and from your evil deeds." (Zech. 1:3–4)

> "Turn to me and be saved, all the ends of the earth! For I am God, and there is no other." (Isa. 45:22)

> "For God has not destined us for wrath, but to obtain salvation through our Lord Jesus Christ, who died for us so

[80] *Roman Catechism*, II, V, 18.
[81] Council of Trent (1551): DS 1674.

> that whether we wake or sleep we might live with him." (1 Thess. 5:9–10)
>
> St. Isidore of Seville states confidently, "All hope consists in confession. Believe it firmly. Do not doubt, do not hesitate, never despair of the mercy of God. Hope and have confidence in confession always."[82]
>
> St. Jerome says, "Do not despair of His mercy no matter how great your sins. For great mercy will take away great sins."[83]

Over the years, I've heard it rightly explained in homilies and talks that the Sacrament of Confession is like spiritual surgery: We expose our wounded heart to Jesus Christ, the Divine Healer and Divine Physician. And the Blessed Virgin Mary, the most perfect model of obedience and faith (see CCC 511), is like the physician's assistant. There is hardly anything better we can do when approaching the Tribunal of Mercy than to clutch our rosary, for example, to remind us of Mary's faithfulness and her role in guiding us to her Son. St. Basil the Great tells us of our Blessed Mother's importance in these matters: "O sinner, be not discouraged, but have recourse to Mary in all your necessities. Call her to your assistance, for such is the divine Will that she should help in every kind of necessity."[84]

Similarly, St. Josemaría Escrivá says, "All the sins of your life seem to be rising up against you. Don't give up hope! On the contrary, call your holy mother Mary, with the faith and abandonment of a child. She will bring peace to your soul."[85]

[82] *Lamentations of a Sinful Soul*, 53.
[83] Commentary on Joel.
[84] Quoted in Johnston, *Voice of the Saints*, chap. 17.
[85] *Friends of God*, 189.

It has also been said that Confession is like regular spiritual maintenance for the soul. Look at it this way: Just as we take a car in for an oil change every few thousand miles, so should we go to Confession to get a tune-up for our spiritual lives. Even if we aren't conscious of mortal sin, a faithful and prayerful monthly Confession keeps our growth in holiness and virtue going smoothly, like a well-maintained engine. Amen to that.

Examination of Conscience and Three Acts of the Penitent

For the penitent, there are four aspects of a proper confession: the *examination of conscience*, followed by what are known as the three acts of the penitent. Regarding the examination of conscience, all seven sacraments require some kind of remote or proximate preparation before they can be received. For the Sacrament of Penance, that proximate preparation is the examination of conscience (see CCC 1454). As each sacrament is truly a *meeting* with the Lord Jesus, we must ready ourselves for that meeting—in the case of Confession, by looking deeply and honestly at our lives so that we come to God with as full an understanding of the state of our souls as possible and ask for pardon.

St. Augustine, in discussing the sin of King David with Bathsheba, relates that asking for pardon for sin is tied to intellectual acknowledgement of sin: "'I acknowledge my transgression,' says David. If I admit my fault, then You will pardon it. Let us never assume that if we live good lives we will be without sin: our lives should be praised only when we continue to beg for pardon."[86]

The three acts of the penitent, then, are *contrition*, *confession*, and *satisfaction*. Regarding contrition, a distinction needs to be made between *perfect* contrition and *imperfect* contrition (also

[86] *Sermo* 19, 2–3: CCL 41, 252–254.

called *attrition*). Perfect contrition is when you are sorry for your sins most of all because they have offended God, Who is all good and deserving of all your love (as one version of the Act of Contrition states). But if you are sorry for your sins and detest them *only* for human motives—for example, because you dread the loss of Heaven and the pains of Hell, or because you've been asked to be a Godparent and the rules require you to be in good standing with the Church—this would be imperfect contrition (attrition). The great news, however, is that Holy Mother Church considers imperfect contrition (that is, a fear of divine justice, even if mixed with human motives) to be a sufficient basis for sorrow for the Sacrament of Confession (see CCC 1451–1453). St. Peter Damien explains this distinction well: "Where there is justice as well as fear, adversity will surely test the spirit. But it is not the torment of a slave. Rather, it is the discipline of a child by its parent."[87]

Second, of course, we have to confess our sins. Confession of one's sins should be done in a simple, concise manner; that is, maintaining the integrity of the confession, yet without going into great and graphic detail about each sin. The following important points were discussed in our first chapter, but because they are so important to making a good, worthy, and reverent confession, they're worth mentioning again here. Mortal sins must be confessed in their kind and approximate number. Any aggravating circumstances that make a mortal sin objectively graver should be included but still mentioned simply—again, without a lot of great or graphic detail.

Remember that venial sins, unlike mortal sins, can be forgiven outside the Sacrament of Confession—by praying a fervent Act of Contrition or by receiving Holy Communion devoutly. Recall that, regarding Confession and forgiveness, God is always our Primary

[87] From a letter by St. Peter Damien, bishop, bk. 8, 6: *PL* 144, 473–476.

Mover, whether or not we are in a state of grace. When we go to Confession or make an Act of Contrition, we are responding to this movement of God's grace in our hearts.

Remember: Confessing venial sins, though not required, is strongly recommended by Holy Mother Church because it helps us fight against evil tendencies and form our consciences properly. "Deliberate and unrepented venial sin disposes us little by little to commit mortal sin" (CCC 1863). God's sanctifying grace comes through the Sacraments, so if we do bring our venial sins to Confession, we can be certain that grace is increased in us.

The third and final act of the penitent that leads to a complete and integral confession is satisfaction, or the proper completion of the assigned penance. Now, keep in mind that the penitent does have the right, if the priest gives a penance that is simply not realistic for his or her state in life—say, a homeschooling mother of seven is told to give several hours of service each week to a soup kitchen—to ask respectfully for an alternative penance. At the same time, the priest has a right to give a penance that is commensurate with the gravity of the sins confessed: In fact, he's duty bound to do that. In most cases, the confessor will give a reasonable and specific penance so that the penitent can be assured that he or she has satisfied it fully.

Several Scripture passages give the wonderful end result of all of this. Psalm 65:2–3 states, "To thee shall all flesh come on account of sins. When our transgressions prevail over us, thou dost forgive them." Deuteronomy 4:29–31 tells us something similar:

> But from there you will seek the LORD your God, and you will find him, if you search after him with all your heart and with all your soul. When you are in tribulation, and all these things come upon you in the latter days, you will return to the LORD your God and obey his voice, for the

> LORD your God is a merciful God; he will not fail you or destroy you.

And Psalm 103:2–3 says simply, "Bless the LORD . . . who forgives all your iniquity." That forgiveness is total and for all time. We must resist the temptation to look back and dwell on sins we have committed but then properly confessed—this kind of obsession can lead to a distrust in God's mercy and love. We are called, very clearly in Scripture, to *move forward*:

> "No one who puts his hand to the plow and looks back is fit for the kingdom of God." (Luke 9:62)

> "One thing I do, forgetting what lies behind and straining forward to what lies ahead, I press on toward the goal for the prize of the upward call of God in Christ Jesus." (Phil. 3:13–14)

> "The dog turns back to his own vomit, and the sow is washed only to wallow in the mire." (2 Pet. 2:22)

> Christ to the woman caught in adultery: "Go, and do not sin again." (John 8:11)

> "Behold, God is my salvation; I will trust, and will not be afraid; for the LORD GOD is my strength and my song, and he has become my salvation." (Isa. 12:2)

That's right: Don't look back on your sins (mortal or venial) that have already been confessed and that have not been recommitted. Move forward. Fr. Jean-Baptiste Rauzan, the founder of my religious community, the Fathers of Mercy, emphasized this trust in God's forgiveness:

> Let us occupy ourselves with the present, leaving the past to the Mercy of God and the future to His Divine Providence.

> If sometimes we recall the past, let it be only to humble ourselves the more, to rouse ourselves up to work in a manner more conformed to the Will and Mind of God.[88]

In His love for us, God calls us to Himself. A primary and ordinary way that He does call us is through the Sacrament of Confession, which can be called by several names that each reveal part of its glory:

> It is called the *sacrament of conversion* because it makes sacramentally present Jesus' call to conversion, the first step in returning to the Father (cf. Mark 1:15; Luke 15:18), from whom one has strayed by sin.
>
> It is called the *sacrament of Penance*, since it consecrates the Christian sinner's personal and ecclesial steps of conversion, penance, and satisfaction.
>
> It is called the *sacrament of confession*, since the disclosure or confession of sins to a priest is an essential element of this sacrament. In a profound sense it is also a "confession"—acknowledgment and praise—of the holiness of God and of his mercy toward sinful man.
>
> It is called the *sacrament of forgiveness*, since by the priest's sacramental absolution God grants the penitent "pardon and peace."[89]
>
> It is called the *sacrament of Reconciliation*, because it imparts to the sinner the love of God who reconciles: "Be reconciled to God" (2 Cor. 5:20). He who lives by God's merciful love is ready to respond to the Lord's call: "Go; first be reconciled to your brother" (Matt. 5:24). (CCC 1423–1424)

[88] Fr. A. De La Porte, SPM, *The Life of the Very Reverend Father Jean-Baptiste Rauzan*, Branigan translation, bk. 5, p. 13.
[89] *Ordo Paenitentiae* 46: formula for absolution.

Indeed, sin is real. But so is God's mercy. And this sacrament of mercy (a sixth title!)—this *Tribunal of Mercy*—is there for the asking for all who seek to overcome sin. If we approach this wonderful sacrament with the mind and the intent that the Church has laid out for us, we will be led to agree with St. Augustine:

> We should be displeased with ourselves when we commit sin, for sin is displeasing to God. Sinful though we are, let us at least be like God in this: that we are displeased at what displeases Him. In some measure, then, you will be in harmony with God's will, because you find displeasing in yourself what is abhorrent to your Creator.[90]

Thank you, St. Augustine, for such a wise counsel.

Now that we've discussed the Sacrament of Penance and Reconciliation at length, let us delve into what, exactly, constitutes proper "fear of the Lord" so as to view God precisely as a loving and merciful Father Who desires that we give Him every aspect of our lives.

[90] Tract. 84, 1–2: CCL 36, 536–538.

Chapter 4

Fear of the Lord and Giving All to God

Put on then, as God's chosen ones, holy and beloved, compassion, kindness, lowliness, meekness, and patience, forbearing one another and, if one has a complaint against another, forgiving each other; as the Lord has forgiven you, so you also must forgive.

—Colossians 3:12–13

O my God, forgive what I have been, correct what I am, and direct what I shall be.

—St. Elizabeth Ann Seton[91]

[91] *Selected Writings*, ed. Ellin Kelly and Annabelle M. Melville (New York: Paulist Press, 1987), 340.

Fear of the Lord

This chapter is about trusting in God's mercy: giving *everything* to Him so that we might feel free to approach that mercy and then extend it to others.

Let's start at the beginning: Who is God? He is a *revealed* God. He is Father, Son, and Holy Spirit: Three Divine Persons in one God, and one God in three Divine Persons. He is the Most Holy, Most Blessed, and Most Adored Trinity. And so, when I say we need to give *everything* to God, I mean our *very lives*: our joys and sorrows, our ups and downs, our successes and failures, our health and ailments, our prayer and work, our recreation and leisure, our injuries received and our forgiveness of injuries, our families and our friendships. Everything. We need to give to God the temporal and spiritual aspects of our lives, the secular and the religious. We need to give all these things to God on a daily basis with a *firm and deliberate act of the will.* He desires this, and this is the primary intention behind the time-honored spiritual practice of making a Morning Offering to God each day upon rising. To better understand this awesome call of "giving everything to God," we have to start with the *proper concept* of "fear of God," or "fear of the Lord." This is important so we can properly understand and establish a relationship with God as loving children who understand fully that we are loved by God.

Scripture is clear that fear of the Lord is essential to our proper relationship with Him:

"With him who fears the Lord it will go well at the end; on the day of his death he will be blessed." (Sir. 1:13)

"Let righteous men be your dinner companions, and let your glorying be in the fear of the Lord." (Sir. 9:16)

"I will give them one heart and one way, that they may fear me for ever, for their own good and the good of their children after them. I will make with them an everlasting covenant, that I will not turn away from doing good to them; and I will put the fear of me in their hearts, that they may not turn from me." (Jer. 32:39–40)

"The fear of the Lord is the beginning of wisdom; a good understanding have all those who practice it." (Ps. 111:10)

"For we are the temple of the living God; as God said, "I will live in them and move among them, and I will be their God, and they shall be my people. Therefore come out from them, and be separate from them, says the Lord, and touch nothing unclean; then I will welcome you, and I will be a father to you, and you shall be my sons and daughters, says the Lord Almighty." Since we have these promises, beloved, let us cleanse ourselves from every defilement of body and spirit, and make holiness perfect in the fear of God. (2 Cor. 6:16–7:1)

So important is "fear of the Lord" that it is also listed as one of the gifts of the Holy Spirit in Isaiah 11:2–3: "The Spirit of the Lord will rest on him—the Spirit of wisdom and of understanding, the Spirit of counsel and of might, the Spirit of the knowledge and fear of the Lord— and he will delight in the fear of the Lord." Note: In the Greek scriptural text, "spirit of Godliness" is also listed and is interpreted as "piety," the seventh gift of the Holy Spirit.

What does fear of the Lord have to do with mercy? St. Athanasius moves us in the right direction: "True joy, genuine festival, means the casting out of wickedness. To achieve this, one must live a life of perfect goodness and, in the serenity of the fear of God, practice contemplation of heart."[92] Serenity and fear? This isn't an intuitive combination. In order to understand it, let's turn to distinctions between different *kinds* of fear.

Proper fear of the Lord is *not* the fear of a cruel master or a dictator. That is *servile* fear, in which the dominant person—the person who is feared—not only has power but ill will. The object of servile fear does not will the good of those over whom he has power; he dominates and subjugates. This is the fear of escaping from wrath, of avoiding punishment, of survival. It is this kind of fear St. John refers to when he writes:

> In this is love perfected with us, that we may have confidence for the day of judgment, because as he is so are we in this world. There is no fear in love, but perfect love casts out fear. For fear has to do with punishment, and he who fears is not perfected in love. We love, because he first loved us. (1 John 4:17–19)

The fear of the Lord we are called to cultivate is quite different—and hinted at in that selection from John's letter. It is *filial* fear, from the Latin *filius*, meaning "son." This is the fear of a son who does not want to offend his father *precisely because he knows his father loves him*; in other words, it's the *fear of not wanting to cause disappointment or give offense*. It is *not* a fear of retribution or punishment. In this proper sense of filial fear, we recognize the infinite gap between us and the Lord, not only in terms of power, *but also* in terms of goodness. We do not fear being annihilated by

[92] An Easter letter, *Liturgy of the Hours*, vol. 2, p. 341.

Him, but we recognize that He could do so if He wished, and in our worship and service we thank Him for His mercy.

This distinction between servile and filial relationships is expressed clearly by St. Paul:

> For you did not receive the spirit of slavery to fall back into fear, but you have received the spirit of sonship. When we cry, "Abba! Father!" it is the Spirit himself bearing witness with our spirit that we are children of God, and if children, then heirs, heirs of God and fellow heirs with Christ, provided we suffer with him in order that we may also be glorified with him. (Rom. 8:15–17)

This can be summed up by St. Francis de Sales, who states clearly and simply, "We must fear God out of love, not love Him out of fear"[93] (i.e., servile fear of God being just a starting point, not the end).

St. Peter Damian emphasizes:

> Where there is justice as well as fear, adversity will surely test the spirit. But it is not the torment of a slave [i.e., servile fear for only human motives]. Rather, it is the discipline of a child by its parent [i.e., servile fear of God moving toward filial fear].[94]

And St. Fulgentius of Ruspe teaches how a proper fear of the Lord can transform our very souls:

> For if any during this life are changed out of fear of God and pass from an evil life to a good one, they pass from death to life and later they shall be transformed from a shameful state

[93] Quoted in Carol Kelly-Gangi, ed., *The Essential Wisdom of the Saints* (New York: Fall River Press, 2008), 7.

[94] From a letter by St. Peter Damien, bishop, bk. 8, 6: *PL* 144, 473–476.

> to a glorious one [i.e., servile fear of God's justice moving toward filial fear and then toward glory].[95]

St. Hilary of Poitiers, a fourth-century bishop, brings it all together with an excellent instruction on the solemn truth that proper filial fear is based on love and is fostered within oneself by a firm and deliberate act of the will. All of this, then, is tied to the gift of wisdom:

> We must begin by crying out for wisdom. We must hand over to our intellect the duty of making every decision. We must look for wisdom and search for it. Then we must understand the fear of the Lord.
>
> "Fear" is not to be taken in the sense that common usage gives it. Fear in this ordinary sense is the trepidation our weak humanity feels when it is afraid of suffering something it does not want to happen. We are afraid, or made afraid, because of a guilty conscience, the rights of someone more powerful, an attack from one who is stronger, sickness, encountering a wild beast, suffering evil in any form. This kind of fear is not taught: it happens because we are weak. We do not have to learn what we should fear: objects of fear bring their own terror with them.
>
> But of the fear of the Lord this is what is written: *Come, my children, listen to me, I shall teach you the fear of the Lord.* The fear of the Lord has then to be learned because it can be taught. It does not lie in terror, but in something that can be taught. It does not arise from the fearfulness of our nature; it has to be acquired by obedience to the commandments, by holiness of life and by knowledge of the truth.
>
> For us the fear of God consists wholly in love, and perfect love of God brings our fear of him to its perfection. Our love

[95] From a treatise on forgiveness.

> for God is entrusted with its own responsibility: to observe his counsels, to obey his laws, to trust his promises.[96]

Here, then, we see the connection between proper fear and mercy. In recognizing that God is *both* infinitely more powerful *and* infinitely more good than we are, we come to understand that His mercy—by which He uses that power for our good—is truly His most wonderful quality. And that mercy is transformative.

Living Right through Prayer

This filial fear of the Lord helps us to understand, also, what it means to live rightly in His eyes. God is our origin and the ultimate end He has destined us for, should we choose it. Everything we do needs to be geared toward that right living, and that is founded on that beautiful fear—yes, fear properly understood can be beautiful!—of a son who does not want to offend his loving father.

The first step in cultivating this proper relationship with the Lord is prayer. After all, what is prayer but communicating with the Trinitarian God? As St. Clement of Alexandria teaches, "Prayer is conversation with God."[97] We are made in God's image and likeness, and wc know through faith that He wants to communicate with us—and so desires that we communicate with Him. What an extraordinary privilege—and, of course, necessity! We know that it is sometimes a struggle to pray, with the distractions of daily life and the constant temptation to ignore God. But let us remember the words of St. Paul: "Likewise the Spirit helps us in our weakness; for we do not know how to pray as we ought, but the Spirit himself intercedes for us with sighs too deep for words"

[96] From a treatise on Psalm 127.

[97] Quoted in Thigpen, *Dictionary of Quotes*, 208.

(Rom. 8:26). During those dry times when prayer does not come easily, it is a great time to remember and acknowledge that we are weak, but it is the Holy Spirit Who makes us strong.

As Christians, we are called to pray in many ways. Of course, there is the high point of earthly prayer: the Mass, the Sacred Liturgy. In fact, Vatican II teaches beautifully that "the Sacred Liturgy is above all things the worship of the Divine Majesty."[98] Outside of this, though, we are called to pray with our spouses, as a family, with our friends, and even, when the time calls for it, with strangers. We are called to pray with Sacred Scripture. We are called to pray with the lives of the saints. We are called to pray with the *Catechism of the Catholic Church*. We are called to renew our baptismal vows in prayer. And through it all, the Holy Spirit is praying for us and wants to lead us into prayer.

Jesus, too, teaches us how to pray to His Heavenly Father, especially in the form of the Lord's Prayer—also known as the Our Father. Note that the first-person pronouns in the Our Father are plural: "Give *us* this day *our* daily bread, and forgive *us* our trespasses as *we* forgive those who trespass against *us*," and so on. This is because man is social by nature, and we relate to God communally, just as surely as we do personally. This is reflected in the public, communal nature of the Mass, at which the Our Father is prayed.

Scripture also tells us something rather intimidating about how we are to pray: "Pray without ceasing" (1 Thess. 5:17, NAB). How can we do this amid the busyness of life? St. Thérèse of Lisieux has the answer: Pick up a pin for the love of God and save a soul.

The young saint, you see, didn't particularly like the needlework she had been assigned in the convent. But instead of grumbling,

[98] Second Vatican Council, Constitution on the Sacred Liturgy *Sacrosanctum Concilium* (December 4, 1963), no. 33.

she decided to dedicate the work to God—even every time she dropped and picked up a pin. This little phrase, then, represents all the little things we do throughout the day—all the little duties we fulfill by our faithfulness to them, all the little and big pieces of work, all the diapers we change, and the sweeping and cleaning of the house, and the office work that we don't enjoy. All these things can be done out of love for God and our neighbor.

Love, Mercy, and the Culture of Death

Love is "the most fundamental and innate vocation of every human being" (CCC 1604). In other words, love is the very core of what it means to be human. This is because our ultimate end is Eternal Beatitude with God, Who *is* Love. St. Bernard of Clairvaux emphasized how love defines our relationship with God: "Of all the movements, sensations, and feelings of the soul, love is the only one in which the creature can respond to the Creator to make some sort of similar return."[99]

For this reason, St. John of the Cross says, "At the evening of life, we shall be judged on our love."[100] This is the love we have for God, which trickles down into our everyday love for our neighbor and, properly ordered, for ourselves. As St. Anthony Mary Claret teaches, "Truly zealous persons are also those who love, but they stand on a higher plane of love. The more they are inflamed by love, the more urgently zeal drives them on."[101] Galatians echoes this by describing just how the "whole law" is fulfilled:

> For you were called to freedom, brethren; only do not use your freedom as an opportunity for the flesh, but through

[99] Sermon 83.
[100] *Dichos* 64, quoted in CCC 1022.
[101] Quoted in Fehrenbach, *Every Day Is Gift*, 155.

> love be servants of one another. For the whole law is fulfilled in one word, "You shall love your neighbor as yourself." (Gal. 5:13–14)

The Letter of James defends this truth about love when it states: "For where jealousy and selfish ambition exist, there will be disorder and every vile practice. But the wisdom from above is first pure, then peaceable, gentle, open to reason, full of mercy and good fruits, without uncertainty or insincerity. And the harvest of righteousness is sown in peace by those who make peace" (3:16–18). Thus, we see in that magnificent document of Vatican II, *Gaudium et Spes*, the reminder that love "is not something to be reserved for important matters, but must be pursued chiefly in the ordinary circumstances of life."[102]

This is, again, our faithfulness to daily duty, whether as a doctor, a farmer, a lawyer, a homeschooling mother of eight, a divorced dad of three striving to live a chaste life, a religious-order priest, a diocesan priest, a cloistered nun within a monastery enclosure, an active religious sister teaching in the classroom, a retired grandparent, a working grandparent, a recently widowed grandparent, a middle school or high school student, a college student, or whatever else we might be called to as part of our vocation and state in life. Love is to be found above all in *everyday life*. Look at it this way: Do what you're supposed to do, when you're supposed to do it, in the way it's supposed to be done. This was the theme of the entire ministry of St. Josemaría Escrivá, the founder of Opus Dei, to teach us that God wants to make saints of us right where we are. Period.

All that said, it's no secret that we are living in an era where there is a tremendous challenge to that vocation of love, and that

[102] Second Vatican Council, Pastoral Constitution on the Church in the Modern World *Gaudium et Spes* (December 7, 1965), no. 38.

is what Pope St. John Paul II called the "Culture of Death."[103] To understand this culture, let's go backward, to the second chapter of the book of Wisdom, which gives the thoughts of an "unrighteous man" who views his life and the world through a nihilistic lens:

> Because we were born by mere chance, and hereafter we shall be as though we had never been; because the breath in our nostrils is smoke, and reason is a spark kindled by the beating of our hearts. When it is extinguished, the body will turn to ashes, and the spirit will dissolve like empty air.... Come, therefore, let us enjoy the good things that exist, and make use of the creation to the full as in youth. Let us take our fill of costly wine and perfumes, and let no flower of spring pass by us. Let us crown ourselves with rosebuds before they wither. Let none of us fail to share in our revelry, everywhere let us leave signs of enjoyment, because this is our portion, and this our lot. (Wisd. 2:2–3, 6–9)

This is nihilism, which is marked by the belief that *nothing* comes after this earthly life. The unrighteous man does not believe in divine justice, so he does not believe in earthly justice. He makes no provision for the afterlife, and so indulges himself in all worldly pleasures without thought of his soul. He ignores, because he has rejected, the Four Last Things: Death, Judgment, Heaven, and Hell. And today we would recognize this person—proving the timeless wisdom of the wisdom literature of the Old Testament—as a secular humanist and a relativist.

This is the philosophy of the Culture of Death: the belief that the human person is the sole arbiter and measure of all things and that this world is all we should, or even can, be concerned about.

[103] Pope St. John Paul II, encyclical letter *Evangelium Vitae* (March 25, 1995), no. 12.

Proponents of the Culture of Death elevate the human will as absolute and pleasure as paramount: These, in the absence of God, are the only things we can trust. And therefore they—and we—have a disordered aversion to suffering. This goes beyond the natural human fear of pain: Any and all adversity is viewed as unbearable. This is because advocates of the Culture of Death have no concept of sharing in the Cross of Jesus Christ. In fact, the Cross looks weak and worthless in this empty philosophy and way of life.

This was foreseen in Sacred Scripture: "Now the Spirit expressly says that in later times some will depart from the faith by giving heed to deceitful spirits and doctrines of demons, through the pretensions of liars whose consciences are seared" (1 Tim. 4:1–2). That phrase, "seared consciences," brings to mind those whose view of right and wrong is malformed by wallowing in the mire of sin, rather than asking God, in His mercy, to heal them of their brokenness. That mercy, as we've said, is God's greatest attribute, which is available to every man and woman for the asking. Nothing is more bittersweet for me as a priest than when a penitent begins his confession by telling me that it has been decades since his last confession (I say this in a hypothetical sense). On the one hand, of course, it's a tremendous blessing to be able to reconcile this soul with God after so many years through His mercy. The prodigal son (or daughter) has returned and is in my midst! He has returned to his Heavenly Father through the wonderful sacrament of mercy—Confession. On the other hand, I'm filled with sadness that this person has deprived himself of God's mercy and the *grace* of the sacraments for so, so long.

The Reality of God's Grace

That grace is mediated through the Church, the Bride of Christ, which He founded to manifest and spread His kingdom throughout the earth. According to the *Catechism*, grace is

> the free and undeserved gift that God gives us to respond to our vocation to become His adopted children. As sanctifying grace, God shares His divine life and friendship with us in a habitual gift, a stable and supernatural disposition that enables the soul to live with God, to act by his love. As actual grace, God gives us the help to conform our lives to his will. Sacramental grace and special graces (charisms, the grace of one's state of life) are gifts of the Holy Spirit to help us live out our Christian vocation.[104]

So, God's grace is given to us as gratuitous favor and makes us participators, as adoptive sons and daughters, in the divine Trinitarian life of God in order that we might become partakers of the divine nature and of eternal life. God's grace is supernatural and is begun in us in the Sacrament of Baptism. But grace doesn't compel us: We have to cooperate with it. Again, as we learned from St. Augustine in chapter 1 and chapter 3: "God created us without us: but he did not will to save us without us." The synthesis of this teaching regarding grace — its initiative and our response — is found in the *Catechism*:

> The *preparation of man* for the reception of grace is already a work of grace. This latter is needed to arouse and sustain our collaboration in justification through faith, and in sanctification through charity. God brings to completion in us what he has begun, "since he who completes his work by cooperating with our will began by working so that we might will it."[105] . . .
>
> God's free initiative demands *man's free response*, for God has created man in his image by conferring on him, along

[104]CCC, glossary, s.v. "grace"; cf. nos. 1996, 2000, 654.
[105]St. Augustine, *De gratia et libero arbitrio*, 17: *PL*, 44, 901.

> with freedom, the power to *know* him and *love* him. The soul only enters freely into the communion of love. God immediately touches and directly moves the heart of man. He has placed in man a longing for truth and goodness that only he can satisfy. The promises of "eternal life" respond, beyond all hope, to this desire. (2001–2002; emphasis added)

A beautiful Scripture quote that sums up the way God's grace works in our lives is in Romans 5, which shows how sanctifying grace can give us the peaceful certitude that we are in God's friendship:

> Therefore, since we are justified by faith, we have peace with God through our Lord Jesus Christ. Through him we have obtained access to this grace in which we stand, and we rejoice in our hope of sharing the glory of God.... And hope does not disappoint us, because God's love has been poured into our hearts through the Holy Spirit who has been given to us. (vv. 1–2, 5)

When it comes to God's grace working in a person's life, St. Thomas Aquinas states simply: "Grace is nothing else but a certain beginning of glory in us."[106] He also teaches about the effects of grace: "First, our soul is healed; second, we will [the] good; third, we work effectively for it; fourth, we persevere; fifth, we break through to glory."[107] And St. Thomas More, the great English husband, father, lawyer, and martyr, says, "Grace is the light by which men see the way to walk out of sin; and grace is the staff without whose help no man is able to rise out of sin."[108] And let's not forget that

[106] Quoted in Thigpen, *Dictionary of Quotes*, 129.
[107] Ibid.
[108] Ibid.

God's grace can also help us to heal our brokenness, as we discussed in the introduction.

Whether sanctifying or actual grace, the Church mediates it on behalf of Her Founder and Bridegroom, Jesus Christ. We believe the Church exists for the glory of God the Father and to enable all men to enter into a relationship with Jesus Christ and thus share in His saving redemption by the power of the Holy Spirit (there's that "Trinitarian spirituality" again!). This is why we call the Church *Holy Mother Church*. Such a task is carried out through the love of a mother who loves her children and wants to see to it that they attain their ultimate end, Eternal Beatitude: communion with God the Father, God the Son, and God the Holy Spirit for all eternity. Amen.

Responding to God's Call

St. Clement of Alexandria, one of the great Fathers of the early Church, wrote this about God's mercy: "The doors are open for all who sincerely and wholeheartedly return to God. Indeed, the Father is most willing to welcome back a truly repentant son or daughter."[109] Of course, this brings to mind the parable of the prodigal son, and Clement continues in reference to the young man's celebrated return:

> Scripture says that for the Father and His Angels in Heaven the festal joy and gladness at the return of just one repentant sinner is great beyond compare.... And so, if you are a thief and desire to be forgiven, steal no more. If you are a robber, return your gains with interest. If you have been a false witness, practice speaking the truth. If you are a perjurer, stop taking oaths. You must also curb all the other evil passions:

[109] Homily on the Salvation of the Rich, 39–40: *PG* 9,644–645.

> anger, lust, grief, and fear. No doubt you will be unable all at once to root out passions habitually given way to, but this can be achieved by God's power, human prayers, the help of your brothers and sisters, sincere repentance, and constant practice.[110]

What beautiful and simple words of hope. Change your life! Get on the path of right living! It doesn't matter what your issues, dependencies, or even addictions to sin are. God, in His love and mercy, calls us constantly to Himself, to better ourselves, to grow in His grace, and to strive to become that "best version of self" that, for each one of us, exists in His divine mind and has for all eternity. What a truth to ponder!

Let's consider some short Scripture passages that respond to our everyday doubts about becoming healed and turning away from sin:

> You say: "I could never reform my life, even if I wanted to." God says, "What is impossible with men is possible with God" (Luke 18:27).
>
> You say, "I'm too tired." God says, "I will give you rest" (Matt. 11:28).
>
> You say, "Nobody really loves me." God says that He loves us (John 3:16; 13:34).
>
> You say, "I can't go on." God says, "My grace is sufficient for you" (2 Cor. 12:9).
>
> You say, "I can't figure things out." God says He will "make straight your paths" (Prov. 3:6).

[110] Ibid.

You say, "I can't do it." God says you "can do all things" (Phil. 4:13).

You say, "It's not worth it." God says, "The sufferings of this present time are not worth comparing with the glory that is to be revealed to us" (Rom. 8:18).

You say, "I can't forgive myself." God says He "will forgive our sins" (1 John 1:9).

You say, "I can't manage it." God says He "will supply every need" (Phil. 4:19).

You say, "I'm afraid." God says He "did not give us a spirit of timidity" (2 Tim. 1:7).

You say, "I don't have enough faith." God says He has given everyone a "measure of faith" (Rom. 12:3).

You say, "I'm not smart enough." God says our wisdom is in Christ Jesus (1 Cor. 1:30).

You say, "I feel all alone." God says, "I will never fail you nor forsake you" (Heb. 13:5).

You say, "I'm always worried and frustrated." God says, "Cast all your anxieties on [me]" (1 Pet. 5:7).

God calls us constantly to Himself because He made us to dwell *in* Him and, eventually, *with* Him in Heaven. This is the source and the meaning of our human dignity. It is what it means to be made in His image and likeness. He is our sole Origin and our sole End, and everything in between should be ordered toward Him through prayer and its fruit, right living. *Your past, no matter how horrendous it was, no longer matters the moment you approach His mercy.*

Be faithful to the sacraments, especially Confession and the Eucharist. Become an active, vibrant, joyful, knowledgeable Catholic, and it will be very possible for you to become a great saint right here in the modern world.

In repentance and holiness is peace and freedom. The psalmist writes: "Blessed is he whose transgression is forgiven, whose sin is covered. Blessed is the man to whom the LORD imputes no iniquity, and in whose spirit there is no deceit" (Ps. 32:1–2). And remember these words of St. Paul:

> And you, who once were estranged and hostile in mind, doing evil deeds, he has now reconciled in his body of flesh by his death, in order to present you holy and blameless and irreproachable before him, provided that you continue in the faith, stable and steadfast, not shifting from the hope of the gospel which you heard, which has been preached to every creature under heaven, and of which I, Paul, became a minister. (Col. 1:21–23)

> But now that you have been set free from sin and have become slaves of God, the return you get is sanctification and its end, eternal life. (Rom. 6:22)

> Of this gospel I was made a minister according to the gift of God's grace, which was given me by the working of his power. To me, though I am the very least of all the saints, this grace was given, to preach to the Gentiles the unsearchable riches of Christ, and to make all men see what is the plan of the mystery hidden for ages in God who created all things; that through the church the manifold wisdom of God might now be made known to the principalities and powers in the heavenly places. This was according to the eternal purpose, which he has realized in Christ Jesus our Lord, in whom we

> have boldness and confidence of access through our faith in him. So I ask you not to lose heart over what I am suffering for you, which is your glory. (Eph. 3:7–13)

You, too, can live in the glory of the saints like St. Paul. The same grace that was given to him, who was a former persecutor and murderer of Christians, is available to you, that you may be its fruit in today's world. Know that God loves you and that you are called to love Him in return, because He calls each one of us personally—and constantly—to Himself.

Spreading God's Mercy

The peace and freedom of God's mercy doesn't simply rest with those whom He forgives—or at least it shouldn't. It's up to us to *extend that mercy to others*, expanding the reign of Christ's love to those around us. St. Caesarius of Arles makes the connection between divine and human mercy:

> Let us make mercy our patroness now, and she will free us in the world to come.... There is ... an earthly as well as heavenly mercy; that is to say, a human and a Divine mercy. Human mercy has compassion on the miseries of the poor. Divine mercy grants forgiveness of sins.[111]

Strictly human mercy may not "grant forgiveness of sins," but it *can* forgive, and it *can* spread Christ's peace to the poor—and not just the poor in material goods, but the poor in spiritual well-being. Of course, we can extend that mercy through specific acts of forgiveness, but we can also cultivate a spirit of Christlike warmth and compassion that imbues all of our relationships and interactions:

[111] Sermon 25.

> Let no evil talk come out of your mouths, but only such as is good for edifying, as fits the occasion, that it may impart grace to those who hear. And do not grieve the Holy Spirit of God, in whom you were sealed for the day of redemption. Let all bitterness and wrath and anger and clamor and slander be put away from you, with all malice, and be kind to one another, tenderhearted, forgiving one another, as God in Christ forgave you.
>
> Therefore be imitators of God, as beloved children. And walk in love, as Christ loved us and gave himself up for us, a fragrant offering and sacrifice to God. (Eph. 4:29–5:2)

The works of mercy illustrate *par excellence* just how it is that each one of us can do our part to help spread God's mercy for the aid and benefit of others. Traditionally, there are fourteen works of mercy: seven for the body, called the Corporal Works of Mercy (from the Latin *corpus*, which means "body"), and seven for the soul, called the Spiritual Works of Mercy. These works of Mercy spring from the Gospel of St. Matthew (25:31–46):

Corporal Works of Mercy
To feed the hungry
To give drink to the thirsty
To clothe the naked
To visit the imprisoned
To shelter the homeless
To visit the sick
To bury the dead

Spiritual Works of Mercy
To admonish the sinner
To instruct the ignorant
To counsel the doubtful

To comfort the sorrowful
To bear wrongs patiently
To forgive all injuries
To pray for the living and the dead

In addition to these, "giving alms to the poor is one of the chief witnesses to fraternal charity: it is also a work of justice pleasing to God."[112] Simply put, the Works of Mercy are "charitable actions by which we come to the aid of our neighbors in their bodily and spiritual needs."[113] While we are able to become beneficiaries of God's mercy especially through the channels of repentance and forgiveness, we need also to be instruments and channels of that same mercy for others—especially since, through God's grace, we become sharers in the divine nature and participators in God's divine life (see 2 Pet. 1:4). He is the One Who gives us His mercy, and He wants us to be cooperators with Him in giving it to others. Note, too, that the works of mercy convey beautifully the reality of the human person as body and soul.

Apart from Sacred Scripture, the writings and wisdom of the saints also echo the importance of cultivating a spirit of Christ that imbues all of our relationships and everyday interactions. For example, regarding the two Spiritual Works of Mercy that exhort us "to bear wrongs patiently" and "to forgive all injuries," St. Cyril of Jerusalem, from a catechetical instruction, teaches us: "If you have a grudge against anyone, forgive him. You are drawing near to receive forgiveness for your own sins; you must yourself forgive those who have sinned against you."[114]

There is in these times a thirst for the truth of Jesus Christ, which will be upheld to the end of time by the Church He founded

[112]CCC 2447; cf. Tob. 4:5–11; Sir. 17:22; Matt. 6:2–4.
[113]CCC, glossary, s.v. "works of mercy"; cf. no. 2447.
[114]*Catechetical Lectures*, 1, 6.

—this same Church that is His Bride and has acted and led visibly in His stead since His Ascension into Heaven and will do so until He comes again at the General Judgment. And this Church, with all of us as Her members, is waging a battle for souls against the devil, who is trying to win as many souls as he can *away* from Almighty God. The demonic Culture of Death wants to deny you, personally, of your divine calling to love and of the mercy of God that love makes available. It does this through exterior forces, but more importantly by tempting us to sin and to believe either that God does not exist or that God does not want the best for us and will not have mercy on us. But of course we can see and experience how much of a lie that is in the great Tribunal of Mercy, the Sacrament of Confession. And it is this same sacrament—regularly received—that sets us on the road to *conversion*, the subject of our next and final chapter.

Chapter 5

Conversion: God Calling Us to Divine Intimacy

Therefore, brethren, be the more zealous to confirm your call and election, for if you do this you will never fall; so there will be richly provided for you an entrance into the eternal kingdom of our Lord and Savior Jesus Christ.

—2 Peter 1:10–11

Do not forget that all the Saints cannot endear you to Christ as much as you can yourself. It is entirely up to you. If you want Christ to love you and help you, you must love Him and always make an effort to please Him. Do not waver in your purpose.

—St. Cajetan[115]

[115] From a letter of the saint.

The Universal Call to Holiness

The call to conversion is nothing less than the universal call to holiness, which was a focal point of the Second Vatican Council.[116] All are called to strive for holiness and truly to be holy, regardless of rank, status, or vocation. In short, all the faithful of Christ are called to the fullness of the Christian life and to the perfection of charity. In responding to God's call to His friendship, we must convert our soul to His service—not once or twice, but every moment of every day. Just as I wrote in my book *The Four Last Things: A Catechetical Guide to Death, Judgment, Heaven, and Hell* that we must strive to live "eternity minded,"[117] so do I believe that we must also strive to live "conversion minded." These two go hand in hand: This is how we join in Christ's victory over sin by overcoming the evil within. St. Paul's Letter to the Ephesians encourages us precisely in this task:

> Put off your old nature which belongs to your former manner of life and is corrupt through deceitful lusts, and be renewed in the spirit of your minds, and put on the new nature, created

[116] Cf. *Lumen Gentium*, chap. 5, "The Universal Call to Holiness in the Church."

[117] Fr. Wade Menezes, CPM, *The Four Last Things: A Catechetical Guide to Death, Judgment, Heaven, and Hell* (Irondale, AL: EWTN Publishing, 2017), 23, 72.

> after the likeness of God in true righteousness and holiness. (Eph. 4:22–24)

And because living "*eternity minded*" and "*conversion minded*" precisely involves the human mind, I like to remind those to whom I preach that the task of conversion—again, the universal call to holiness—requires fervent "intellectual seeking" of God and "willful choosing" of Him. Dorothy Day, a cofounder of the Catholic Worker movement, echoes this when she states the following:

> We have the great and glorious gift of free will, which distinguishes man from the beast, the power of choice, and man often chooses evil because it has the semblance of the good, because it seems to promise happiness.... To grow in faith in God, in Christ, in the Holy Spirit, that is the thing. Without Him we can do nothing. With Him we can do all things.[118]

Let's spend some time diving into what the *Catechism of the Catholic Church* has to say about conversion:

> Jesus calls to conversion. This call is an essential part of the proclamation of the Kingdom. "The time is fulfilled, and the Kingdom of God is at hand; repent, and believe in the Gospel" (Mark 1:15).... It is by faith in the Gospel and by Baptism (cf. Acts 2:38) that one renounces evil and gains salvation, that is, the forgiveness of all sins and the gift of new life.
>
> This endeavor of conversion is not just a human work. It is the movement of a "contrite heart," drawn and moved

[118]Dorothy Day, *The Reckless Way of Love: Notes on Following Jesus* (Walden, NY: Plough Publishing House, 2017), 11.

> by grace to respond to the merciful love of God who loved us first. (1427–1428)[119]

Origen, the early Church theologian, put it bluntly: "The Kingdom of God cannot exist alongside the reign of sin."[120] As we've said throughout this book: God is always the Primary Mover in helping us to overcome sin and its allure in our lives. It requires our humble contrition, which is our openness to being emptied of our sinful attachments and filled by God's goodness. Later in the *Catechism*, we read how the first step to this conversion, like anything else, is recognizing the problem:

> "Conversion *requires convincing of sin*; it includes the interior judgment of conscience, and this, being a proof of the action of the Spirit of truth in man's inmost being, becomes at the same time the start of a new grant of grace and love."[121] (1848)

If we're not convinced of the reality of sin and its devastating consequences, we can't experience conversion. By its very nature, conversion requires that we *know* that we are broken and need the help that only God can provide to heal us. We don't have to have a perfect knowledge of our sins but enough to begin the process of leaning on God's goodness and mercy.

This conversion isn't a last step in the process of God's grace healing us; it's the very first step: "The first work of the grace of the Holy Spirit is *conversion*" (CCC 1989). Pope St. Leo the Great tells us that "all must therefore strive to ensure that on the day of redemption no one may be found in the sins of his former life."[122]

[119] Quoting Psalm 51:17; cf. John 6:44; 12:32; 1 John 4:10.
[120] *Notebook on Prayer*, chap. 25: *PG* 11, 495–499.
[121] Pope St. John Paul II, *Dominum et Vivificantum*, 31 § 2.
[122] *Sermo 6 de Quadragesima*, 1–2: *PL* 54, 285–287.

We are reminded here what a gift we have in the Sacrament of Penance and Reconciliation, which pours out God's grace on us in a special way, reviving our friendship with Him and allowing us truly to put our past behind us. In other words, who you've been is *not* who you have to be.

Grace, Virtue, and Conscience

Under the heading "The Virtues and Grace," the *Catechism* teaches:

> Human virtues acquired by education, by deliberate acts and by a perseverance ever-renewed in repeated efforts are purified and elevated by divine grace. With God's help, they forge character and give facility in the practice of the good. (CCC 1810)

The virtues—that is, the habits of choosing *for* rather than *against* God's truth and goodness—are both the fruit of our conversion and the way we maintain its momentum over time: "Man of God, shun all this; aim at righteousness, godliness, faith, love, steadfastness, gentleness. Fight the good fight of the faith; take hold of the eternal life to which you were called" (1 Tim. 6:11–12). We are called, with God's help, to partake every day of the true and the good, versus the false and the evil. The *Catechism*, however, follows this with a note of caution: "It is not easy for man, wounded by sin, to maintain moral balance" (1811). We talked in chapter 2 about how easy it is for the passions to be knocked out of balance, especially if we lack the self-knowledge to understand where they are leading us astray. But in conversion to Christ, there is help:

> Christ's gift of salvation offers us the grace necessary to persevere in the pursuit of the virtues. Everyone should always ask for this grace of light and strength, frequent the

> sacraments, cooperate with the Holy Spirit, and follow his calls to love what is good and shun evil. (CCC 1811)

Here we see some concrete ways—which we will expand on later in this chapter—to make the grace of conversion part of our lives. Take advantage, especially, of every opportunity to receive sacramental grace, especially in Eucharist and Confession, which are the two sacraments that can be received again and again. This sanctifying grace—of which the seven sacraments are the ordinary channels—makes us participators in God's divine life. This truth was mentioned earlier, but it can't be stressed enough; sanctifying grace is such a gift! This is the road to conversion: striving for the good against evil, with the grace of the sacraments showing us the way.

> If we truly think of Christ as our source of holiness, we shall refrain from anything wicked or impure in thought or act and thus, show ourselves to be worthy bearers of His Name for the quality of holiness is shown, not by what we say necessarily but by what we do in life.[123]

All of this leads also to the very special grace of a clear conscience. In the book of Acts, we read St. Paul's response after having been dragged before the council for his preaching of Christ: "Brethren, I have lived before God in all good conscience up to this day" (23:1). If we could only say that when we make our general examination of conscience at the end of the day! Think of the old maxim: "A clear conscience makes the best pillow." In the clear conscience—the sure knowledge that we have followed God's plan for us this day—is genuine and beautiful Christian peace. And in this peace, we can hear God's call all the more clearly to live a devout life:

[123] St. Gregory of Nyssa, *Christian Perfection*.

> And you, who once were estranged and hostile in mind, doing evil deeds, he has now reconciled in his body of flesh by his death, in order to present you holy and blameless and irreproachable before him. (Col. 1:21–22)

> Now may the God of peace who brought again from the dead our Lord Jesus, the great shepherd of the sheep, by the blood of the eternal covenant, equip you with everything good that you may do his will, working in you that which is pleasing in his sight, through Jesus Christ; to whom be glory for ever and ever. Amen. (Heb. 13:20–21)

We hear about this peace at every Mass, after the Lord's Prayer, when the priest quotes the words of Christ to His Apostles: "Peace I leave with you; my peace I give to you" (John 14:27). In other words, Our Lord wants to give us His peace; He doesn't want us to fall to pieces because of an unconverted heart, an unconverted mind, or an unconverted life.

Setting ourselves on the path of conversion by recognizing and combatting sin, by living an active sacramental life, and by accepting God's gift of virtue, we are on our way to becoming a great saint. This way of living then serves to increase the faith we've already accepted: Each step in the right direction increases our momentum. We never rest on our laurels, but rather "let us run with perseverance the race that is set before us" (Heb. 12:1). Therefore, we should want to nurture faith, and all the virtues. Stagnant virtues quickly atrophy: We need to practice them in prayer (such as the acts of faith, hope, and charity) and deed (such as the Corporal and Spiritual Works of Mercy).

Part of conversion, then, is witnessing to the truth of the Faith in our lives. Scripture says, "The righteous shall live by his faith" (Hab. 2:4, referenced in Rom. 1:17; Gal. 3:11; Heb. 10:38). And in Luke 18:8, Christ asks us hauntingly, "When the Son of man comes, will he find faith on earth?" The gift of conversion, like all the gifts of God, is meant to be shared.

Witnessing Our Conversion

Each one of us has been given a sphere of influence. As the Second Vatican Council put it, "The obligation of spreading the faith is imposed on every disciple of Christ, according to his state.... Upon all the laity, therefore, rests the noble duty of working to extend the divine plan of salvation to all men of each epoch and in every land."[124] Pope St. John Paul II put it this way: "The witness of a Christian life well lived is the first and irreplaceable form of mission"[125] This is the life we are called to by Christ through our Baptism and Confirmation, sustained by regular Eucharist and Penance: to be a great evangelizer of the faith. The *Catechism* doesn't mince words, connecting our evangelizing mission with the "clear conscience" described by St. Paul:

> Before Pilate, Christ proclaims that he "has come into the world, to bear witness to the truth" (John 18:37). The Christian is not to "be ashamed then of testifying to our Lord" (2 Tim. 1:8). In situations that require witness to the faith, the Christian must profess it without equivocation, after the example of St. Paul before his judges. We must keep "a clear conscience toward God and toward men" (Acts 24:16). (2471)

This is all part of the universal call to holiness, in which we are invited into divine intimacy, with Christ as our Model.

> The duty of Christians to take part in the life of the Church impels them to act as *witnesses of the Gospel* and of the

[124]*Lumen Gentium*, 17, 33.
[125]Pope St. John Paul II, *Redemptoris Missio* (December 7, 1990), 32.

> obligations that flow from it. This witness is a transmission of the faith in words and deeds. Witness is an act of justice that establishes the truth or makes it known. (CCC 2472; cf. Matt. 18:16)

Your faithful presence in the lives of those around you—that is, those whom God has placed in your life—is a form of evangelization that will help establish the truth in the modern world. This is your "sphere of influence." We are, the *Catechism* goes on, strengthened by the sacraments in this noble undertaking:

> All Christians by the example of their lives and the witness of their word, wherever they live, have an obligation to manifest the new man, which they have put on in Baptism and to reveal the power of the Holy Spirit by whom they were strengthened at Confirmation. (2472)[126]

Acts 18 tells us that St. Paul was dragged into court and charged with influencing people to worship God. What a marvelous blemish to have on one's record! The chapter continues with these words of Our Lord to St. Paul: "Do not be afraid. Go on speaking and do not be silenced for I am with you." (vv. 9–10)

What a dignified task we have, to be faithful to our vocation in the time and place God has given us. And this faithfulness to our vocation, the fruit of conversion, will make us saints.

The Business of Sanctity

It's one thing to understand the necessity of conversion, but it's another to take the practical steps to make it an ongoing reality in our lives. With that in mind, I want to suggest several spiritual habits

[126] Quoting Second Vatican Council, Decree on the Missionary Activity of the Church *Ad Gentes* (December 7, 1965), no. 11.

and devotional practices we can all integrate into our lives in order to access and cooperate with the grace that makes conversion possible.

The Sacramental Life

As we've discussed, the seven sacraments are the ordinary channels through which we receive God's sanctifying grace, which makes us participators in His divine life. Therefore, the following are ever so important: monthly Confession, weekly Eucharist, and, if possible, daily Mass — or, at least attending Mass occasionally during the week. Additionally, it can be wonderfully fruitful to make a weekly visit to the Blessed Sacrament for adoration — hopefully a Holy Hour, but if not a full hour, then at least a fifteen-minute visit at a local parish church. As Catholics, we have in the sacramental life of the Church an incredible treasury of riches. And we have a responsibility to take advantage of these riches, to make them part of our lives, and therefore to bring their abundance to the world.

St. Albert the Great wrote straightforwardly: "Anyone who receives the Sacrament [of the Eucharist] with the devotion of sincere faith will never taste death."[127] What a wonderful, faith-filled incentive to draw ever closer to this "source and summit of the Christian life."[128]

Basic Books

There are four texts that should be in every Catholic home — and I don't mean stored away in the attic or resting unopened in a guest bedroom; I mean out in the open and *used* as part of the everyday life of the family. This is by no means an exhaustive list of such texts, but four that can aid greatly in the task of conversion.

[127] *Commentary on the Gospel of St. Luke.*
[128] *Lumen Gentium*, 11.

The Bible

Try to read one chapter a day. It might sound intimidating, but most chapters take less than five minutes to read. If you add some quiet meditation afterward, which is always great to do when reading Scripture, it can take a bit longer. And you don't have to start at the beginning: The Gospels are a great place to start, and then maybe the Epistles, or some of the Wisdom books of the Old Testament, such as the book of Proverbs. There's no substitute for the Word of God.

The Catechism of the Catholic Church

Throughout this book, we've quoted from this wonderful text, which brings together two thousand years of wisdom in Sacred Scripture, Tradition, and the Magisterium (the teaching office of the Church). Each paragraph is numbered and takes only a minute or two to read. Read a few paragraphs a day, and in no time, you'll begin to know your faith better. Here's an important suggestion: Never sit down with the *Catechism* without a highlighter or a brightly colored pen or marker. You'll definitely want to take note of beautiful passages or challenging topics to examine more in depth, or a cross-reference to Scripture to come back to later.

Lives of the Saints

Get a good, condensed collection of the lives of the saints, in which each saint's story is only a page or two. Read one a week, maybe on the weekend, focusing on those saints who shared the same state in life as you (e.g., as a mother, a father, a priest). We benefit from reading about all the saints and how they practiced virtues and honored God in the circumstances of their everyday lives, but remember: Those saints who are similar to us in their vocations and states in life can especially inspire us.

The Diary of St. Faustina

St. Faustina was the first saint canonized in the Great Jubilee Year 2000 and thus also the first saint canonized in the third millennium. John Paul II intentionally held off on all canonizations early in that year because he wanted the focus of the new millennium to be on mercy. So it was that St. Faustina was canonized on Divine Mercy Sunday, the week after Easter, because it was from her visions, writings, and advocacy that the celebration existed at all. St. Faustina's diary, *Divine Mercy in My Soul*, can truly be considered one of the greatest works of mystical literature in the two-thousand-year history of the Church. That's good enough reason for me to keep the book around! I recommend, as with the *Catechism*, reading a few numbered paragraphs each day.

Habits of Prayer

St. Teresa of Avila is said to have remarked, "It is impossible for a person who prays regularly to remain in serious sin; because the two are incompatible; one or the other will have to be given up." With this important truth in mind, let's now look at some good habits (virtues!) of prayer that can help to make conversion a major part of our lives. Remember: Who you've been is *not* who you have to be. Conversion is possible, ready for the asking and taking.

The Rosary

John Paul II, to commemorate the beginning of his silver jubilee as pope, promoted the Rosary in a wonderful letter titled, simply, *The Rosary of the Virgin Mary* (*Rosarium Virginis Mariae*). It was here that he proposed five new mysteries to be prayed on the beads: the Luminous Mysteries, which focus on events from Christ's public ministry. In this letter, Pope John Paul II described the Rosary as:

> a prayer loved by countless Saints and encouraged by the Magisterium. Simple yet profound, it still remains, at the dawn of this third millennium, a prayer of great significance, destined to bring forth a harvest of holiness. It blends easily into the spiritual journey of the Christian life, which, after two thousand years, has lost none of the freshness of its beginnings.[129]

Although there are traditionally fifteen decades of Hail Marys in an entire Rosary (five each in the Joyful, Sorrowful, and Glorious Mysteries), and twenty today with the addition of the Luminous Mysteries, it remains the norm to pray five decades at a time. That is a reasonable expectation for a daily devotion, as well. But if you find yourself in a state of life in which you have the freedom to take on the entire Rosary (for example, those who are homebound), John Paul writes (and I agree!) that it would be a beautiful and heroic act to do so. The benefits of practicing such a closeness to the Mother of God is echoed by St. Bernard of Clairvaux, Doctor of the Church:

> May her name never be far from your lips, or far from your heart.... If you follow her, you will not stray; if you pray to her, you will not despair; if you turn your thoughts to her, you will not err. If she holds you, you will not fall; if she protects you, you need not fear; if she is your guide, you will not tire; if she is gracious to you, you will surely reach your destination.[130]

Another Marian prayer that can be prayed on its own, or at the conclusion of the Rosary, is the Litany of the Blessed Virgin Mary, also known as the Litany of Loreto. This recitation of the titles of Our Lady can be found in appendix B.

[129] Pope St. John Paul II, apostolic letter *Rosarium Virginis Mariae* (October 16, 2002), no. 1.

[130] St. Bernard of Clairvaux, *In laudibus Virginis Matris*, Homily 2, 17.

The Divine Mercy Chaplet

Prayed on rosary beads, the Divine Mercy Chaplet comes from the visions of St. Faustina Kowalska, a Polish nun. Begin the Chaplet with one Our Father, one Hail Mary, and the Apostles' Creed. Then, on the "Our Father" beads, pray the "Eternal Father" prayer: "Eternal Father, I offer you the Body and Blood, Soul and Divinity of Your dearly beloved Son, Our Lord, Jesus Christ, in atonement for our sins and those of the whole world." On the "Hail Mary" beads, pray this Divine Mercy prayer: "For the sake of His sorrowful Passion, have mercy on us and on the whole world." Conclude by praying three times: "Holy God, Holy Mighty One, Holy Immortal One, have mercy on us and on the whole world." The Chaplet is a short, deeply meditative devotion that takes only about seven minutes to pray.

Examinations of Conscience

We've discussed this earlier in the book, so here we'll only briefly review. First, it is good to make a short, particular examination of conscience at midday, perhaps focusing on a specific virtue you are trying to advance in your life, or, a specific vice that you are trying to root out. Then, at the end of the day, make a general examination of your conscience, looking over your whole day, and closing with an Act of Contrition. The Confiteor ("I confess to Almighty God and to you, my brothers and sisters . . .") from Mass could serve as your Act of Contrition and would allow you to end each day with a liturgical prayer from the celebration of the Eucharist, which is a comforting thought and a wonderful practice!

Spiritual Shout-Outs

One form of prayer that often gets overlooked are short "spiritual shout-outs"—sometimes called "aspirations"—that we can make throughout the day. An example would be to say, whether regularly throughout the day, or when faced with any of the several little challenges that arise daily: "My Jesus, mercy." Maybe you say this fifteen, twenty, or twenty-five times a day: Those are dozens of little affirmations of God's love and mercy in our lives. Here are a few more, some of which have a call-and-response aspect that could allow you to include your spouse or children:

Give thanks to the Lord for He is good.
His mercy endures forever.

Our help is in the name of the Lord,
Who made heaven and earth.

O Mary, conceived without sin,
Pray for us who have recourse to thee.

This is the day the Lord has made.
Let us rejoice and be glad.

My guardian angel, protect me.

Jesus, Mary, and Joseph, I love you; save souls.

Mary, my Mother, never abandon me.

Immaculate Heart of Mary, pray for me.

Most Sacred Heart of Jesus, have mercy on me.

My Lord Jesus Christ, make me a saint.

Pick one of these and stick with it throughout the day or the week or the month. It's a beautiful habit to form, and it will keep your mind and heart on God. In other words, such aspirations will help you to practice the "presence of God" throughout the day. Here are a few more ideas to help strengthen your spiritual life:

- † *Each time you pass a Catholic Church*, pray: "O Sacrament Most Holy, O Sacrament Divine, all praise and all thanksgiving, be every moment Thine." In doing so, you are both acknowledging and honoring the Real Presence of Our Lord Jesus Christ truly present in the Most Blessed Sacrament—the Holy Eucharist—in His Body, Blood, Soul, and Divinity.
- † *Each time you pass a cemetery*, pray: "Eternal rest grant unto them, O Lord, and let perpetual light shine upon them. May their souls and all the souls of the faithful departed, through the mercy of God, rest in peace. Amen." Here, you are offering a commemoration of all those who have died, commending them to the mercy of God.

Because these are all so short, they can be easily memorized and made into regular habits. Walking in the grocery store, putting on your seat belt, making breakfast for your kids: These are all moments that can be sanctified with these short, fervent, aspirations. Each time you pray them, you are making an *act of the will* to bring yourself into God's presence.

Be sure to refer to appendix A for other essential short prayers, including an Act of Contrition and Acts of Faith, Hope, and Love that you can memorize and make a regular part of your spiritual life.

Staying Faithful

These spiritual exercises do require a certain amount of commitment and discipline. For some, a more strictly regimented approach might make sense—not the kind of thing that makes you neurotic or scrupulous, but rather, a simple regularization of your prayerful habits. For others, these prayerful practices may come more naturally, and so such persons are able to keep them a part of their regular prayer life more easily, without regimentation.

Simply look at your current daily habits and figure out when is the best time of day to add prayer—for parents, it might be before the kids wake up or after they go to bed; for others, it might be during commutes or at lunchtime. Times when it's dark, or quiet, or otherwise boring (traffic jams) might fit the bill. The important thing is to make the commitment and then to keep it, and in a short time, you won't be able to imagine your life without these spiritual exercises.

Yet, it does take effort to stay *faithful* to these kinds of exercises. This is because the body and soul are intimately linked. On days when the soul isn't feeling especially fervent, the body will also slow down and respond more favorably to, say, watching TV than talking to God. During these lethargic moments, we need to make a deliberate and fervent act of the will that will get the body and soul in line, actively choosing for God so that the next time, the choice will, God willing, be easier to make. An early Christian priest, in a second-century homily, teaches us how such acts of the will can lead us to virtue and help us, at the same time, to be truly sorry for sin:

> For the sake of eternal life, my brothers, let us do the will of the Father Who called us, resisting the temptations that lead us into sin and striving earnestly to advance in virtue.... We should blot out past sins by being truly sorry for them, and then we shall be saved.[131]

God and Man

> In Jesus Christ God not only speaks to man but also seeks him out. The Incarnation of the Son of God attests that

[131] Attributed to a "Pseudo-Clement of Rome."

> God goes in search of man.... It is a search which begins in the heart of God and culminates in the Incarnation of the Word.[132]

This is how Pope St. John Paul II describes the meaning of the Incarnation in his 1994 document in anticipation of the third millennium, *Tertio Millennio Adveniente*. The Incarnation is an act of God's "coming to" man. He takes on our human nature while retaining His Divine Personage, demonstrating that God goes out to man in order to draw man to Himself. And to this day and through the end of time, through the Holy Spirit and the Church, the Bride of Christ, God constantly calls us to Himself. We can know this precisely because He came to us. As quoted earlier, in chapter 4:

> For we are the temple of the living God; as God said, "I will live in them and move among them, and I will be their God, and they shall be my people." Since we have these promises, beloved, let us cleanse ourselves from every defilement of body and spirit, and make holiness perfect in the fear of God. (2 Cor. 6:16; 7:1)

St. Faustina recorded in her diary these remarkable words of the Lord that describe the reality that we are indeed meant to be temples of God:

> I want to pour out My divine life into human souls and sanctify them, if only they were willing to accept my grace. The greatest sinners would achieve great sanctity, if only they would trust in My mercy.... My delight is to act in a

[132]Pope St. John Paul II, apostolic letter *Tertio Millennio Adveniente* (November 10, 1994), no. 7.

> human soul and to fill it with My mercy and to justify it. My kingdom on earth is My life in the human soul. (1784)

Wow. Jesus is telling us, through His revelations to St. Faustina, that His kingdom *on* earth *is* His life *in* the human soul. He draws us *to* the Father *in* the Holy Spirit. Christianity teaches that God searches for man, leading him, as Scripture so often depicts it, into the quiet of the desert to speak to him in the silence of his heart. Christianity sees God as a personal and loving God Who calls the human creature to Himself. We believe that it is the Trinitarian God Who has chosen us, not we who have chosen Him. God is always the Primary Mover. Jesus says exactly this to the Apostles: "You did not choose me, but I chose you" (John 15:16).

Each one of us can say, "God has called me to Him." He has done this by giving us His Son, sending Him Incarnate in a manger in Bethlehem, and He has also given us the Church, born as the Bride of His Son from His Son's side on the Cross. And essential to that call from Him is the call to His Church, to remain loyal sons and daughters of Holy Mother Church. Thus, we are and remain loyal brothers and sisters of Jesus Christ, and loving sons and daughters of the Father, while we beseech the Holy Spirit to enter into and transform our lives.

God calls us constantly to Himself by giving us His love, and He yearns as Father, Son, and Holy Spirit for our love for Him. Pope St. Leo the Great tells us:

> The good and chaste soul is so happy to be filled with Him that it desires to take delight in nothing else. For what the Lord says is very true: "Where your treasure is, there also will your heart be."[133]

[133] *Sermo* 92, 1.2.3: *PL* 54, 454–455.

Bold Holiness in the Saints and Blesseds

A well-grounded life of prayer and conversion brings with it a bold holiness. We see this, for example, in the lives of the saints and blesseds of the Church.

Nec laudibus, nec timore: "Neither by praise, nor by fear." This was the episcopal motto of Blessed Cardinal Clemens August Graf von Galen, the Archbishop of Münster, Germany, from 1933 to 1946 during the reign of Adolf Hitler. Von Galen was a strong and forthright critic of the Nazi regime, and he denounced forcefully the Third Reich's euthanasia programs and its persecution of the Catholic Church. Within Germany, he stood as one of the most prominent figures of opposition against the Nazi party and its programs and policies, including the deportation and extermination of Jews. He was declared Venerable by Pope John Paul II in 2003 and beatified by Pope Benedict XVI two years later. That episcopal motto—"Neither by praise, nor by fear"—defined his life and work in the challenging circumstances of Hitler's Germany: Neither by praise nor by fear would he be swayed from his duties and separated from God. He was faithful to his office and to his vocation.

Consider another World War II Catholic icon: St. Edith Stein, the holy Carmelite philosopher nun whose name in religious life was Teresa Benedicta of the Cross. All her life, Edith sought truth—from her Jewish roots, to agnosticism (some scholars would say a practical atheism), to the study of philosophy, then to a flirtation with Protestantism, and finally to the fullness of truth in Catholicism. Her journey of faith and reason culminated in her becoming a Carmelite nun. In both her philosophical and religious writings, she delved into the meaning of human suffering. Throughout the process of her continued scholarship and maturing intellectual thought she sought to grow in greater intimacy with God. As an ethnic Jew, she was evacuated to the Netherlands, but the Church could no longer protect her after the Dutch bishops condemned Hitler, and the Nazi authorities took her to Auschwitz. With her older sister Rosa, Edith died in the gas chambers. She was beatified and declared a saint by Pope John Paul II, who, in 1999, declared her one of the three co-patronesses of Europe, along with Bridget of Sweden and Catherine of Siena.

These modern holy people of God teach us that He wants to make us each a saint right where we are, even amid persecution. "Blessed is the man who endures trial, for when he has stood the test he will receive the crown of life which God has promised to those who love him" (James 1:12). St. Augustine says about the diversity of vocations, and thus the diversity of holiness:

> I tell you again and again, my brethren, that in the Lord's garden are to be found not only the rose of his martyrs. In it there are also the lilies of the virgins, the ivy of wedded couples, and the violets of widows. On no account may any class of people despair thinking that God has not called them. Christ suffered for all. What the Scriptures say of Him is true. He desires all men to be saved and to come to the knowledge of the truth.[134]

And St. Paul writes in his famous teaching on the variety of the gifts of the Spirit:

> Now there are varieties of gifts, but the same Spirit; and there are varieties of service, but the same Lord; and there are varieties of working, but it is the same God who inspires them all in every one. To each is given the manifestation of the Spirit for the common good. To one is given through the Spirit the utterance of wisdom, and to another the utterance of knowledge according to the same Spirit, to another faith by the same Spirit, to another gifts of healing by the one Spirit, to another the working of miracles, to another

[134] *Sermo* 304, 1–4: *PL* 38, 1395–1397.

> prophecy, to another the ability to distinguish between spirits, to another various kinds of tongues, to another the interpretation of tongues. (1 Cor. 12:4–10)

Indeed, God wants to make you a saint right there where you are, and He wants to use the gifts He has given you — elevated by a big helping of grace — to make it happen. It's up to each of us, though, to accept this royal invitation and turn to Him. Thus, Pope St. Leo the Great tells us, "The business of this life should not preoccupy us with all of its anxiety and pride that we no longer strive with the love of our heart to be like Our Creator, Our Redeemer, and to follow His example."[135] Finally, St. Paul tells us where our strength truly lies:

> Be strong in the Lord and in the strength of his might. Put on the whole armor of God, that you may be able to stand against the wiles of the devil. For we are not contending against flesh and blood, but against the principalities, against the powers, against the world rulers of this present darkness, against the spiritual hosts of wickedness in the heavenly places. Therefore take the whole armor of God that you may be able to withstand in the evil day, and having done all, to stand. (Eph. 6:10–13)

Freedom

Ultimately, conversion is an exercise of one's freedom both interiorly and exteriorly. The choice is ours to make. In the *Catechism*, the student of faith is treated to a wonderful section on the freedom of the human person, which is rooted in his or her human dignity. Here are some of the chief paragraphs of that section:

[135] Sermon 66, 3–4.

> Freedom is the power, rooted in reason and will, to act or not to act, to do this or that, and so to perform deliberate actions on one's own responsibility. By free will one shapes one's own life. Human freedom is a force for growth and maturity in truth and goodness; it attains its perfection when directed toward God, our beatitude.
>
> As long as freedom has not bound itself definitively to its ultimate good which is God, there is the possibility of *choosing between good and evil*, and thus of growing in perfection or of failing and sinning. This freedom characterizes properly human acts. It is the basis of praise or blame, merit or reproach.
>
> The more one does what is good, the freer one becomes. There is no true freedom except in the service of what is good and just. The choice to disobey and do evil is an abuse of freedom and leads to "the slavery of sin." (cf. Rom. 6:17). (1731–1733)

Here are just a couple of the many Scripture passages that echo beautifully these teachings on human freedom:

> For you were called to freedom, brethren; only do not use your freedom as an opportunity for the flesh, but through love be servants of one another. For the whole law is fulfilled in one word, "You shall love your neighbor as yourself." (Gal. 5:13–14)

> But now that you have been set free from sin and have become slaves of God, the return you get is sanctification and its end, eternal life. (Rom. 6:22)

Part of *growing in virtue*, then, is *growing in freedom*, because true freedom is found only in Christ. Too often in our culture, we are told that freedom is the ability to do whatever we want, but this is a dangerous lie. While we can choose, in freedom, to ignore God, sin never enhances our freedom: It only enslaves us to our passions and other attachments.

Growing in virtue, on the other hand, allows us to overcome these barriers to authentic freedom by habituating us, quite simply, to choosing to be free by choosing to follow Christ. Thus, through a robust spiritual life that forms our free will always to seek the true and the good and the beautiful, we can move toward our ultimate end: union with God. The process of conversion, then, is one of bringing our will into accordance with God's will.

And there is where our ultimate freedom lies—the freedom of peace and serenity and a clear conscience that comes with embracing God's love and grace. As Fr. Jean-Baptiste Rauzan puts it: "And you, God's friends, from now on, no more anxiety, no more alarm, because all the favors of [Divine] Providence are for you."[136] In other words, God wishes to bestow His divine favors upon us, His friends.

Life, my friends, is a journey toward God. And the beautiful truth is that He gives us all the tools necessary to draw close to Him—and to overcome the evil within—*right now*.

And so, we have everything we need to move forward confidently, because in entering into a relationship with Christ, we have entered into the process of overcoming sin. We begin, as we did in this book, by understanding and accepting sin's reality and its consequences, but that's not the end of the story: God's grace and mercy are ready to transform us, to *free us* from slavery to sin. Through prayer and the sacraments and the hard—but rewarding—work of growing in self-knowledge, virtue, fear of the Lord, and conversion, we work with God to put ourselves on the path of salvation.

[136] Fr. A. De La Porte, SPM, *The Life of the Very Reverend Father Jean-Baptiste Rauzan*, Quinn translation, bk. 1, p. 13.

Appendices

Appendix A

Daily Prayers

Act of Faith

O my God, I firmly believe that You are one God in three Divine Persons, Father, Son and Holy Spirit. And I believe that Your Divine Son, Jesus, became man and died for our sins, and that He will come again to judge the living and the dead. I believe these and all the truths that the holy Catholic Church teaches, because You have revealed them, O God, Who can neither deceive nor be deceived. Amen.

Act of Hope

O my God, relying on Your almighty power and infinite mercy and promises, I hope to obtain pardon of my sins, the help of Your grace, and life everlasting, through the merits of Jesus Christ, my Lord and Redeemer. Amen.

Act of Charity

O my God, I love You above all things, with my whole heart and soul, because You are all good and deserving of all my love. I love my neighbor as myself for the love of You. I forgive all those who have injured me, and I ask pardon of all those whom I have injured. Amen.

Act of Contrition

O my God, I am heartily sorry for having offended You, and I detest all my sins because I dread the loss of Heaven and the pains of Hell; but most of all, because they have offended You, my God, Who are all good and deserving of all my love. I firmly resolve, with the help of Your grace, to confess my sins, to do penance, and to amend my life. Amen.

Memorare

Remember, O most gracious Virgin Mary, that never was it known that anyone who fled to your protection, implored your help, or sought your intercession was left unaided. Inspired by this confidence, I fly unto you, O Virgin of virgins, my Mother; to you do I come, before you I stand, sinful and sorrowful. O Mother of the Word Incarnate, despise not my petitions, but in your mercy, hear and answer me. Amen.

Appendix B

LITANY OF THE BLESSED VIRGIN MARY

V. Lord, have mercy on us,
R. Christ, have mercy on us.
V. Lord, have mercy on us; Christ hear us,
R. Christ, graciously hear us.

God, the Father of heaven, *have mercy on us.*
God, the Son, Redeemer of the world, *have mercy on us.*
God, the Holy Spirit, *have mercy on us.*
Holy Trinity, one God, *have mercy on us.*

Holy Mary, *pray for us.*
Holy Mother of God, *pray for us.*
Holy Virgin of virgins, *pray for us.*
Mother of Christ, *pray for us.*
Mother of the Church, *pray for us.*
Mother of mercy, *pray for us.*
Mother of divine grace, *pray for us.*
Mother of hope, *pray for us.*
Mother most pure, *pray for us.*
Mother most chaste, *pray for us.*
Mother inviolate, *pray for us.*
Mother undefiled, *pray for us.*

Mother most amiable, *pray for us.*
Mother most admirable, *pray for us.*
Mother of good counsel, *pray for us.*
Mother of our Creator, *pray for us.*
Mother of our Savior, *pray for us.*
Virgin most prudent, *pray for us.*
Virgin most venerable, *pray for us.*
Virgin most renowned, *pray for us.*
Virgin most powerful, *pray for us.*
Virgin most merciful, *pray for us.*
Virgin most faithful, *pray for us.*
Mirror of justice, *pray for us.*
Seat of wisdom, *pray for us.*
Cause of our joy, *pray for us.*
Spiritual vessel, *pray for us.*
Vessel of honor, *pray for us.*
Singular vessel of devotion, *pray for us.*
Mystical rose, *pray for us.*
Tower of David, *pray for us.*
Tower of ivory, *pray for us.*
House of gold, *pray for us.*
Ark of the covenant, *pray for us.*
Gate of Heaven, *pray for us.*
Morning star, *pray for us.*
Health of the sick, *pray for us.*
Refuge of sinners, *pray for us.*
Comforter of migrants, *pray for us.*
Comforter of the afflicted, *pray for us.*
Help of Christians, *pray for us.*
Queen of angels, *pray for us.*
Queen of patriarchs, *pray for us.*
Queen of prophets, *pray for us.*

Queen of Apostles, *pray for us.*
Queen of martyrs, *pray for us.*
Queen of confessors, *pray for us.*
Queen of virgins, *pray for us.*
Queen of all saints, *pray for us.*
Queen conceived without original sin, *pray for us.*
Queen assumed into Heaven, *pray for us.*
Queen of the Most Holy Rosary, *pray for us.*
Queen of families, *pray for us.*
Queen of peace, *pray for us.*

Lamb of God, who takest away the sins of the world,
spare us, O Lord.
Lamb of God, who takest away the sins of the world,
graciously hear us O Lord.
Lamb of God, who takest away the sins of the world,
have mercy on us.

V. Pray for us, O holy Mother of God.
R. That we may be made worthy of the promises of Christ.

Let us pray: Grant, O Lord God, we beseech Thee, that we Thy servants may rejoice in continual health of mind and body; and, through the glorious intercession of Blessed Mary ever Virgin, may be freed from present sorrow, and enjoy eternal happiness. Through Christ our Lord. Amen.

Appendix C

LITANY OF THE SACRED HEART OF JESUS

V. Lord, have mercy.
R. Lord, have mercy.
V. Christ, have mercy.
R. Christ, have mercy.
V. Lord, have mercy.
R. Lord, have mercy.
V. Christ, hear us.
R. Christ, hear us.
V. Christ, graciously hear us.
R. Christ, graciously hear us.

God the Father of Heaven,
have mercy on us.
God the Son, Redeemer of the world,
have mercy on us.
God, the Holy Spirit,
have mercy on us.
Holy Trinity, One God,
have mercy on us.

Heart of Jesus, Son of the Eternal Father,
have mercy on us.

Heart of Jesus, formed by the Holy Spirit in the womb of the Virgin Mother, *have mercy on us.*

Heart of Jesus, substantially united to the Word of God, *have mercy on us.*

Heart of Jesus, of Infinite Majesty, *have mercy on us.*

Heart of Jesus, Sacred Temple of God, *have mercy on us.*

Heart of Jesus, Tabernacle of the Most High, *have mercy on us.*

Heart of Jesus, House of God and Gate of Heaven, *have mercy on us.*

Heart of Jesus, burning furnace of charity, *have mercy on us.*

Heart of Jesus, abode of justice and love, *have mercy on us.*

Heart of Jesus, full of goodness and love, *have mercy on us.*

Heart of Jesus, abyss of all virtues, *have mercy on us.*

Heart of Jesus, most worthy of all praise, *have mercy on us.*

Heart of Jesus, King and center of all hearts, *have mercy on us.*

Heart of Jesus, in Whom are all treasures of wisdom and knowledge, *have mercy on us.*

Heart of Jesus, in Whom dwells the fullness of divinity, *have mercy on us.*

Heart of Jesus, in Whom the Father was well pleased, *have mercy on us.*

Heart of Jesus, of Whose fullness we have all received, *have mercy on us.*

Heart of Jesus, desire of the everlasting hills,
have mercy on us.
Heart of Jesus, patient and most merciful,
have mercy on us.
Heart of Jesus, enriching all who invoke Thee,
have mercy on us.
Heart of Jesus, fountain of life and holiness,
have mercy on us.
Heart of Jesus, propitiation for our sins,
have mercy on us.
Heart of Jesus, loaded down with opprobrium,
have mercy on us.
Heart of Jesus, bruised for our offenses,
have mercy on us.
Heart of Jesus, obedient to death,
have mercy on us.
Heart of Jesus, pierced with a lance,
have mercy on us.
Heart of Jesus, source of all consolation,
have mercy on us.
Heart of Jesus, our life and resurrection,
have mercy on us.
Heart of Jesus, our peace and our reconciliation,
have mercy on us.
Heart of Jesus, victim for our sins,
have mercy on us.
Heart of Jesus, salvation of those who trust in Thee,
have mercy on us.
Heart of Jesus, hope of those who die in Thee,
have mercy on us.
Heart of Jesus, delight of all the saints,
have mercy on us.

Lamb of God, who takest away the sins of the world,
spare us, O Lord.
Lamb of God, who takest away the sins of the world,
graciously hear us O Lord.
Lamb of God, who takest away the sins of the world,
have mercy on us.

V. Jesus, meek and humble of heart.
R. Make our hearts like to Thine.

Let us pray: Almighty and eternal God, look upon the Heart of Thy most beloved Son and upon the praises and satisfaction which He offers Thee in the name of sinners; and to those who implore Thy mercy, in Thy great goodness, grant forgiveness in the name of the same Jesus Christ, Thy Son, who livest and reignest with Thee forever and ever. Amen.

About the Author

Fr. Wade L. J. Menezes, CPM, is a member of the Fathers of Mercy, a missionary preaching religious congregation based in Auburn, Kentucky. Ordained a priest during the Great Jubilee Year 2000, he received his Bachelor of Arts Degree in Catholic Thought from the Oratory of St. Philip Neri in Toronto, Canada, and his dual Master of Arts and Master of Divinity Degrees in Theology from Holy Apostles Seminary in Cromwell, Connecticut. His secular college degrees are in journalism and communications.

Fr. Wade is currently the Assistant General of the Fathers of Mercy and has served as Director of Vocations and Director of Seminarians for the congregation. He has also served as the Chaplain-in-Residence at the Shrine of the Most Blessed Sacrament of Our Lady of the Angels Monastery in Hanceville, Alabama. While at the shrine, Fr. Wade was a daily Mass celebrant, homilist, and confessor; he also gave spiritual conferences on specialized points of Catholic doctrine to the many pilgrims who visited the shrine.

Fr. Wade has been a contributing writer for the *National Catholic Register*, *Our Sunday Visitor*, *Catholic Twin Circle*, *Lay Witness*, *Pastoral Life*, and *Christian Ranchman*. Several of his homiletic series have appeared in *Homiletic and Pastoral Review*, an international journal for priests. Fr. Wade has also been a guest on EWTN's *Mother Angelica Live* and *Life on the Rock* programs, during which he discussed topics such as the sanctification of marriage and family life, vocations, and the Sacred Liturgy. He has hosted several series for EWTN, including *Crux of the Matter*, *The Wonders of His Mercy*, *The Ten Commandments of Catholic Family Life*, *The Four Last Things*, *God Calls Us to Himself*, and *The Gospel of Life versus the Culture of Death*. Many of his theological presentations have been featured on EWTN Catholic Radio, Ave Maria Radio, Covenant Network, Guadalupe Radio Network, and Mater Dei Radio. His first book for EWTN Publishing is *The Four Last Things: A Catechetical Guide to Death, Judgment, Heaven, and Hell.*